Math for Real Life
Practical Math for Teens and Beyond

Math for Real Life
Practical Math for Teens and Beyond

Published by
Heron Books, Inc.
20950 SW Rock Creek Road
Sheridan, OR 97378

heronbooks.com

Special thanks to all the teachers and students who
provided feedback instrumental to this edition.

Fourth Edition © 1985, 2024 Heron Books
All Rights Reserved

ISBN 978-0-89-739269-3

Any unauthorized copying, translation, duplication or distribution, in whole or in part, by any means, including electronic copying, storage or transmission, is a violation of applicable laws.

The Heron Books name and the heron bird symbol are registered trademarks of Delphi Schools, Inc.

14 July 2024

At Heron Books, we think learning should be engaging and fun. It should be hands-on and allow students to move at their own pace.

To facilitate this we have created a learning guide that will help any student progress through this book, chapter by chapter, with confidence and interest.

Get learning guides at
heronbooks.com/learningguides.

For teacher resources,
such as a final exam, email
teacherresources@heronbooks.com.

We would love to hear from you!
Email us at *feedback@heronbooks.com.*

CONTENTS

Part 1
Getting Started

1 What Is Math for Real Life? 3
    Getting Started 4

2 Mental Math 5
    Problem-Solving Strategy 6
    Addition 7
        Exercise 1 10
    Subtraction 11
        Exercise 2 14
    Multiplication 14
        Exercise 3 17
        Exercise 4 18
    Division 18
        Exercise 5 20
    Percents 21

Part 2
Math for Money

3 Investing Money 25
    Banks and Credit Unions 25
    Bonds 26
    Stocks 26
    Property 27

	Interest	27
	Inflation	28

4 Figuring Out Interest 29
Computing Simple Interest 29
    Exercise 1 30
Interest Compounded Annually 30
    Exercise 2 31
Compound Interest with Savings Added Annually 31
Interest Compounded Other Than Annually 32
    Exercise 3 32
Compound Interest with Savings Added Monthly 33
    Exercise 4 34
Real Life 34

5 Borrowing Money 37
Simple Loans 37
Installment Loans 38
    Exercise 1 41
Credit Cards 42
Rules for Successful Borrowing 43
    Exercise 2 44
Finance Charges 44

6 Taxes 45
Sales Tax 45
    Exercise 1 46
Income Taxes 46
Property Taxes 48
    Exercise 2 48
Other Taxes 48

Part 3
Math for Measuring

7 Measuring Different Ways 51
    Units 52
        Exercise 1 54
    Inverses 55
        Exercise 2 55
    Combined Units 56
    Summary 58
        Exercise 3 58

8 Useful Formulas 59
    Rate Formula 60
        Exercise 1 61
    Mileage Formula 61
        Exercise 2 62
    Electrical Energy 62
        Exercise 3 64
    Temperature Conversions 65
        Exercise 4 66
    Ratios & Proportions 67
        Exercise 5 69

Part 4
Math for Statistics and Probability

9 Statistics 73
    Trends 73
    Scale 75

	What Is Being Compared	76
	Other Kinds of Graphs	77
	Exercise 1	80
	Averages	80
	Exercise 2	82
	Errors in the Data	82
	Correlation	84
	Exercise 3	84
	Exercise 4	85

10 Probability 87

Methods of Stating Probabilities 87
    Exercise 1 89
    Exercise 2 89
Computing Probabilities 90
The Meaning of Probability 95
Probability and Statistics 96
    Exercise 3 97
    Exercise 4 97

11 Closing 101

    Exercise 1 101

Appendix 103

Getting Started Exercises 105
Answers to Getting Started Exercises 109
Answers to Problems and Exercises 111

Part 1

Getting Started

Chapter 1
What Is Math for Real Life?

Most of us use math every day in lots of ways—at the grocery store, at the gas station, figuring how much time until an appointment, finding out the chances that it's going to rain on an important day. Math is nothing more than the language we use to think about and talk about exact amounts of things such as money, time, distance, and so on. "It costs $32.95," "that's 14 gallons," "the appointment is in 25 minutes," "there's an 80% chance of rain."

You might be so good at that kind of math that you hardly even think of it as math. But what happens when you run into something a little more complicated, like deciding whether to accept that credit card offer? How much will it *really* cost to use that card?

Here are some real-life examples of when you'll want your math to be up to the job.

- You're buying shoes and you want to compare the prices of two pairs that are on sale. Which is less expensive: the $125 shoes on sale for 35% off, or the $95 shoes on sale for $10 off?

- You're planning a vacation in Europe, where distances are measured in kilometers, but you're used to judging distances in miles. How do you change from one way of measuring to the other?

WHAT IS MATH FOR REAL LIFE?

- You are buying a car that costs $20,800. Since you do not have that much money saved, you get a car loan. Now you have payments of $384.00 per month for five years, which includes some money to the bank for giving you the loan. After two years, you get some extra money and decide to pay off the car loan. How much money would this save you?

- Someone has told you that if you put $1,000.00 in savings at 8% interest compounded annually and leave it there for 20 years, you will be a millionaire. Is this true? (*Compound interest* will be covered in Chapter 4.)

This book is meant to put you in control of the math you'll need for real life. It's not meant to teach you, say, how to do your taxes or where to invest money. But it's meant to make you certain that you've got the math you need to survive in the everyday world of being an adult.

GETTING STARTED

To get the most out of this book, you will need some basic math skills. A set of exercises has been provided in the appendix that will give you a chance to verify these, or brush up on anything needed. See "Getting Started Exercises" on page 105.

Chapter 2
Mental Math

One of the first tricks to using math in real life is being able to quickly work out the math in your head. Do I have enough money? Do I have enough gas for this trip? What if I need just 1/3 of this recipe?

Often when you need to figure something out using math, you do it on the fly without writing it down or using a calculator. In this chapter, you'll get some tips on doing math quickly in your head. In later chapters, you will get the chance to use your mental math in real-life situations.

Solving math problems "in your head" can be useful in a situation like this:

You are in the checkout line at the grocery store and suddenly realize you have only $30.00 available. You have about 30 seconds before it's your turn. These items are in your cart:

Bread	$5.09
Milk	$4.83
Hamburger	$6.64
Butter	$4.87
Pickles	$3.19
Dozen donuts	$9.39

Do you have enough money to pay for them?

MENTAL MATH

PROBLEM-SOLVING STRATEGY

Here are some steps that you would take to solve any mental math problem.

1. Look over the data to get an idea of the type of answer you are looking for.

2. Decide whether to solve with addition, subtraction, multiplication, or division.

3. Decide how accurate the answer should be and whether rounding and estimating will be quicker and give an answer that is close enough.

4. Look for a way to make the math easier by rounding or breaking down a number into simpler parts.

5. If more accuracy is needed, get it by unrounding at the end.

You can get really fast at mental math by starting with easy problems and just practicing lots!

The mental arithmetic part of mental problem solving depends mainly on the ability to do simple math in your head. There are some tricks that can help you. Once you get good at mental arithmetic, mental problem solving will seem like the natural thing to do in many situations.

MENTAL MATH

ADDITION

Do it from left to right. This allows you to round the numbers. At each point, you can decide if the answer is close enough or if you need more accuracy.

For example, to do this problem,

$$\begin{array}{r} 137 \\ + 385 \\ \hline \end{array}$$

think of it as

$$\begin{array}{r} 100 + 30 + 7 \\ +300 + 80 + 5 \end{array}$$

First add the hundreds, then tens, then ones.

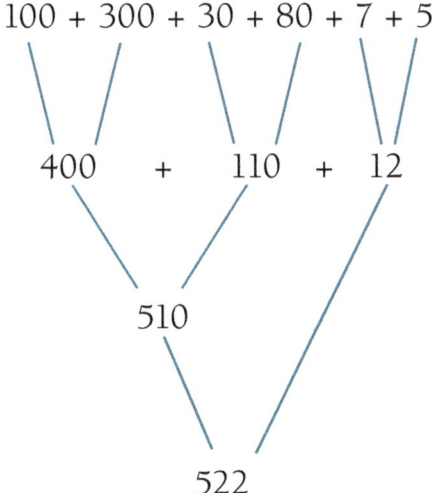

With practice, you will just add the hundreds plus tens plus ones like this.

400 + 110 = 510 + 12 = 522

For this problem,

$$\begin{array}{r} 485 \\ + 376 \\ \hline \end{array}$$

think 700 ⇨ 850 ⇨ 861. The answer is 861.

7

MENTAL MATH

To do this quickly, you need to know basic math facts well. That way there is no hesitation in noticing that 8 + 7 = 15 (therefore 80 + 70 = 150).

For some problems, there is another shortcut.

In this problem

$$\begin{array}{r} 85 \\ + 39 \\ \hline \end{array}$$

notice that 39 is 1 less than 40. 85 + 40 is 125, so, 85 + 39 will be one less than 85 + 40, or 124.

Look at this problem:

$$\begin{array}{r} 128 \\ + 68 \\ \hline \end{array}$$

68 is 2 less than 70, and 128 + 70 is 198. So the answer to this is 2 less than 198, or 196. Or you could round both 128 and 68 and add 130 + 70 = 200. Since 128 is 2 less than 130, and 68 is 2 less than 70, the answer is 4 less than 200, or 196.

The above is useful when the last digit of a number is 8 or 9.

When the last digit is 1 or 2, you can round that digit down at first, then "unround" at the end.

$$\begin{array}{r} 145 \\ + 72 \\ \hline \end{array}$$

Here you have 145 + 70 = 215, plus 2 = 217.

Finally, when adding money, notice when a sum is equal to or almost equal to 100, as in this problem.

$$\begin{array}{r} \$2.27 \\ +4.73 \\ \hline \end{array}$$

If you notice that 27 + 73 = 100, then the answer is clearly $7.00.

$$\begin{array}{r} \$8.37 \\ +4.64 \\ \hline \end{array}$$

Notice that 36 + 64 equals 100, so 37 + 64 must be 101. Then the answer is

$$12.00 + 1.01 = \$13.01$$

Mental arithmetic like this takes some practice, but you will find that you have lots of opportunities to practice it in everyday life. And once you get used to doing it, you'll find it saves you lots of time—and people will think you're a math whiz!

MENTAL MATH

Exercise 1

Do each problem mentally and write down your answer. Use rounding and unrounding or other tricks where they help.

Add these problems mentally.

1. 24 + 54
2. 26 + 53
3. 89 + 24
4. 87 + 28
5. 35 + 78
6. 132 + 57
7. 234 + 75
8. 356 + 35
9. 356 + 167
10. $2.14 + $5.64
11. $5.34 + $.89
12. $7.68 + $2.32
13. $2.34 + $.69 + $1.76 + $3.11 + $.45
14. $1.56 + $2.45 + $.36 + $1.19 + $3.67
15. $10.66 + $15.34 + $11.85 + $22.60

Problem #1

Now that you know some addition tricks, how would you answer this problem using mental math?

You are in the checkout line at the grocery store and suddenly realize you have only $30.00 available. You have about 30 seconds before it's your turn. These items are in your cart:

Bread	$5.09
Milk	$4.83
Hamburger	$6.64
Butter	$4.87
Pickles	$3.19
Dozen donuts	$9.39

Do you have enough money to pay for them?

Answers are in the appendix.

SUBTRACTION

There are similar tricks for subtraction problems. For example:

$$\begin{array}{r} 147 \\ - 94 \\ \hline \end{array}$$

It's easier to subtract 100 than 94, so mentally round 94 to 100. 147 − 100 = 47. You can then unround by adding 6 to get 53.

Or you could add the same amount to both numbers. Because 147 + 6 is 153, the problem above becomes 153 − 100 with answer 53.

MENTAL MATH

In the following problem

$$\begin{array}{r} 254 \\ -85 \\ \hline \end{array}$$

One way would be to add 15 to 85 to make it 100. Then you can easily subtract 254 − 100 = 154. Next, fix your answer by adding 15 to 154, to get 169.

You could also do it this way:

$$\begin{array}{r} 843 \\ -\,179 \\ \hline \end{array}$$

Decide which number is closest to the nearest ten or hundred. Since adding 21 to 179 makes 200, start there.

When you increase both numbers by 21, the problem becomes
864 − 200 = 664.

For problems in the thousands, see if it's easy bringing it to the nearest thousand, ten or hundred.

$$\begin{array}{r} 6920 \\ -\,5865 \\ \hline \end{array}$$

By adding 135, it becomes 6000.

Add 135 to both numbers

$$\begin{array}{r} 7055 \\ -\,6000 \\ \hline 1055 \end{array}$$

This method depends on your ability to do mental addition to the nearest 10, 100, 1000, and so on.

It's easy to subtract when the last digits of both numbers are the same.

$$\begin{array}{r} 157 \\ -77 \\ \hline 80 \end{array}$$

To make the following problem easier, adjust one of the numbers so the last numbers match, then adjust the answer. For example,

$$\begin{array}{r} 183 \\ -44 \\ \hline \end{array}$$

Here you can adjust 44 to 43. Then you have 183 – 43, which is 140. Then subtract 1 from 140, so the answer is 139. This is a lot like the rounding-unrounding trick, but instead of rounding to 0 you match the last digits.

If the problem were,

$$\begin{array}{r} 185 \\ -44 \\ \hline \end{array}$$

you could add 1 to 44 and have

$$\begin{array}{r} 185 \\ -45 \\ \hline 140 \end{array}$$

then add 1 to get 141.

MENTAL MATH

Exercise 2

Subtract these problems mentally.

1. 55 – 24
2. 87 – 26
3. 98 – 64
4. 83 – 25
5. 143 – 35
6. 198 – 39
7. 120 – 46
8. 110 – 62
9. 245 – 134
10. 324 – 245
11. 945 – 783
12. 1500 – 387
13. 1234 – 156
14. 2330 – 1234
15. 4350 – 1265

MULTIPLICATION

One digit by two or more digits

The basic way to multiply one digit by two or more digits is to break the larger number down into hundreds, tens, and ones, multiply each, then add the result.

$$8 \cdot 43 = 8 \cdot (40 + 3) = 8 \cdot 40 + 8 \cdot 3 = 320 + 24 = 344$$

As with addition you can work from left to right. That will give you a rough answer quickly, and you can refine it as you go. With practice, you won't think through all of the steps to yourself.

$$7 \cdot 254 = 7 \cdot (200 + 50 + 4)$$
$$= 1400 + 350 + 28 = 1778$$
$$1400 \Rightarrow 1750 \Rightarrow 1778$$

By 10

To multiply by 10 just add a zero.

$$24 \cdot 10 = 240$$

By 5

To multiply by 5, you can multiply by 10, then take half.

$$5 \cdot 72 = \text{half of } 10 \cdot 72 = \text{half of } 720 = 360$$

Or if you are multiplying 5 times an even number, take half. Then multiply it by ten.

$$5 \cdot 72 = 10 \cdot \text{half of } 72 = 10 \cdot 36 = 360$$

If you are multiplying 5 times an odd number, it is easier to multiply by 10 first.

You decide which way you prefer.

By 15

To multiply by 15, first multiply by 10, then take half of that answer and add it to the first.

$$15 \cdot 84 = ?$$
$$10 \cdot 84 = 840, \text{ half of } 840 \text{ is } 420, 840 + 420 = 1260$$

By 25

To multiply by 25, add two zeros, take ½, then take half again:

	25 · 54
Add two zeros:	5400
Take half:	2700
Take half again:	1350

MENTAL MATH

Multiplying 2 digits by 2 digits

$$\begin{array}{r} 34 \\ \times\ 27 \\ \hline \end{array}$$

There are a few different ways to approach this type of problem. The one that works most often is to break 27 into 20 + 7, and multiply each by 30 and 4, then add the answer.

$20 \cdot 30 = 600,\ 20 \cdot 4 = 80,\ 600 + 80 = 680$

$7 \cdot 30 = 210$

$7 \cdot 4 = 28$

$680 + 210 + 28 = 918$

If you don't think out each operation, it would be:

680 ⇨ 890 ⇨ answer 918.

Here's another one.

$$\begin{array}{r} 83 \\ \times\ 17 \\ \hline \end{array}$$

$10 \cdot 83 = 830$

$+\ 7 \cdot 80 = 560$

$+\ 7 \cdot 3 = 21$

$830 + 560 + 21 = 1411$

Or 830 ⇨ 1390 ⇨ answer 1411.

If the number you are multiplying by has 9 as the last digit:

$$\begin{array}{r} 54 \\ \times\ 39 \\ \hline \end{array}$$

Notice that 39 + 1 is 40. Multiplying by 40 is easier.

4 · 54 = 216, so 40 · 54 = 2160

Then you do 2160 − 54 = 2106.

You could think 2160 ⇨ 2106.

It is up to you to decide which number is being multiplied by which. For example, look at this problem.

$$\begin{array}{r} 25 \\ \times\ 47 \\ \hline \end{array}$$

It would be easier to multiply 47 by 25 by the "multiplying by 25 method." 4700 ⇨ 2350 ⇨ answer 1175.

Exercise 3

Multiply these problems mentally.

1. 2 × 81
2. 6 × 19
3. 4 × 34
4. 7 × 23
5. 3 × 56
6. 8 × 73
7. 5 × 32
8. 5 × 47
9. 5 × 53
10. 9 × 68

MENTAL MATH

Exercise 4

Multiply these problems mentally.

1. 15 × 24
2. 15 × 34
3. 25 × 84
4. 25 × 15
5. 14 × 21
6. 36 × 28
7. 49 × 64
8. 67 × 15
9. 52 × 41
10. 73 × 95

DIVISION

In any division problem where you are dividing by more than one digit, there isn't a trick to it. You just do multiplication mentally. For example, look at this division problem.

You're driving to Salt Lake City and pass a sign saying you have 300 kilometers to go. You're traveling at 90 kilometers per hour and have an appointment in the city in 3½ hours. Will you arrive on time?

$$300 \div 90 = ?$$

You guess the answer is about 3 hours, so you multiply 3 × 90 mentally to get 270. This leaves 30, which means that after 3 hours you will have 30 kilometers to go. Since your appointment is in 3½ hours, you have ½ hour to go 30 kilometers, which you could do if you were going only 60 kilometers per hour. That means you'll arrive before 3½ hours and be on time for your appointment.

This trick is just a way of estimating and rounding to get an answer that is close enough.

MENTAL MATH

There are a few tips that are helpful when dividing by certain one-digit numbers:

Dividing by 2, 4, or 8

To divide by 2, you take half. To divide by 4 you take half twice, and to divide by 8 you take half three times.

$$180 \div 2 = \tfrac{1}{2} \text{ of } 180 = 90$$

$$180 \div 4 = \tfrac{1}{2} \text{ of } \tfrac{1}{2} \text{ of } 180 = \tfrac{1}{2} \text{ of } 90 = 45$$

$$180 \div 8 = \tfrac{1}{2} \text{ of } \tfrac{1}{2} \text{ of } \tfrac{1}{2} \text{ of } 180 = \tfrac{1}{2} \text{ of } \tfrac{1}{2} \text{ of } 90 = \tfrac{1}{2} \text{ of } 45 = 22.5$$

Dividing by 5

To divide by 5, divide by 10 and multiply that by 2.

$$95 \div 5 = ?$$

$$95 \div 10 = 9.5 \cdot 2 = 19$$

$$95 \div 5 = 19$$

Or you can multiply by 2 first and then divide by 10.

$$95 \div 5 = ?$$

$$95 \cdot 2 = 190 \div 10 = 19$$

$$95 \div 5 = 19$$

MENTAL MATH

Sometimes dividing by a two-digit number is easier by noticing that a multiple of the divisor would give you a simpler problem. For example, to divide 350 by 25 you might notice that by mentally doubling 25 you have 50. That divides into 350 to give 7. Then multiply 7 by 2 to get the correct answer.

$$350 \div 25 = ?$$
$$350 \div 50 = 7$$
$$7 \cdot 2 = 14$$
$$350 \div 25 = 14$$

Exercise 5

Divide these problems mentally (estimate as needed).

1. 156 ÷ 2
2. 384 ÷ 4
3. 940 ÷ 4
4. 2480 ÷ 8
5. 670 ÷ 5
6. 295 ÷ 5
7. 180 ÷ 30
8. 365 ÷ 52
9. 270 ÷ 45
10. 357 ÷ 45
11. 360 ÷ 15
12. 356 ÷ 55

MENTAL MATH

PERCENTS

It comes in handy to be able to figure out percents mentally every time you need to figure out a tip for some service.

Say you have a meal in a restaurant and your bill is $44.00. The restaurant recommends a 20% tip for your waiter and you need to add it before you pay for your meal. An easy way to figure this is take 10% of $44.00 and multiply that answer by 2.

First, it's very easy to find 10% of any number by just moving the decimal point of the number one place to the right. For example. 10% of $24.50 is $2.45. 10% of $8.00 is $.80 (80¢).

So 20% of $44.00 = ?

10% of $44.00 = $4.40

$4.40 · 2 = $8.80

20% of $44.00 is $8.80 tip

Total of meal with tip = $44.00 + 8.80 = $52.80

Problem #2

You have had a great meal at a nice restaurant with a friend. The total bill is $92.00, and your part is $47.00. You want to give your waitress a 20% tip. Mentally figure what the total for your meal and the tip would be.

Part 2

Math for Money

Chapter 3
Investing Money

Investing means using money to earn more money.

There are different ways to invest money, all with the goal of earning more money. Any investment also has some risk of losing some or all the money you invested. Usually, the safer your money is, the less it will earn. On the other hand, when there is more risk in an investment, there are potentially more rewards.

Let's look at ways to invest money.

BANKS AND CREDIT UNIONS

The most common way to save money is to put it in a bank savings account to earn interest. **Interest** is the money someone pays for the use of someone else's money. This is covered more fully later.

In banks your savings are insured up to a certain amount by the Federal Deposit Insurance Corporation. The risk is low, but so is the reward.

A credit union is much like a bank, but it may pay you for the use of your money in another way. Every three months, or quarter, the money earned by the credit union from those who borrow from it is divided up among those who have money saved. Thus, you receive a percentage of the profits. These are called **dividends**, from the word "divide." Savings in credit unions are also insured up to a certain amount.

INVESTING MONEY

BONDS

When a government or corporation wants to raise money, they may issue a bond. A **bond** is a piece of paper that promises the issuer will return the loaned money by a certain date, called the maturity date, with interest.

There are different types of bonds offered in denominations (or amounts) from $50 to $1,000,000. Depending on the type of bond, it may mature, or become payable, in 1 to 30 years. The longer you wait, the more money your investment earns for you.

If you want to get your money back from a bond before it matures, you can sell it to another person who could then hold it to maturity.

Government bonds are usually a safe investment because the government guarantees the money will be paid back. Corporate bonds work the same way, but both the risk and the interest promised may be higher.

STOCKS

When you buy shares of **stock** in a company, you have part ownership in the company and are entitled to a share of its earnings. The company uses the money from sales of stock to expand its business.

Stocks of profit-making companies pay dividends from their profits. For instance, if you own 50 shares of a company and the company pays a dividend of 25 cents per share, you receive $12.50.

You can also make money if the value of the stock goes up, or appreciates and you can sell it at the higher price. For instance, you might buy the stock for $25 for each share, and later sell it at $27.50 per share. You don't actually receive that money until you sell the stock.

A new company that is not making a profit yet might sell shares of its stock but not pay dividends. This is a higher-risk investment because you make money only if the company succeeds. With an established company, the stock might not appreciate fast, but you earn dividends as a low-risk investment.

INVESTING MONEY

PROPERTY

You can also try to make money by buying things that you can sell at a profit later. Some people buy real estate, diamonds, gold, or fine art that they think will gain in value.

By comparing the initial investment and the eventual return, you can judge whether the interest rate on your investment justifies the risk of losing your money.

INTEREST

Interest works like this: You deposit $100 in the bank. The bank keeps some of the money, and loans out the rest. By loaning out the money, the bank earns interest. Part of this goes to you as interest on your deposit, and the bank keeps the rest for operating expenses and profit.

The interest you earn is figured as a percentage of the money you have in savings, which is computed and added to your savings at regular intervals of time. For example, a bank may advertise 4% interest yearly. If you have $200 in savings for one year, then at the end of that year the bank adds in another 4% of $200, which is $8 (0.04 × $200 = $8), and you have $208.

The initial savings is called the **principal**, the percentage used to calculate interest is called the **interest rate**.

It makes a difference how often the bank computes your interest. Suppose in the example given that your interest on the $200 savings was computed every 6 months instead of yearly. Remember that the interest rate is 4% each year—that doesn't change. At the end of 6 months, the bank pays you 4% × $200 × ½, since the money has been in for ½ year. This is $4. You now have $204 in savings. This is your new principal. At the end of another 6 months, interest is again computed: 4% × $204 × ½ = $4.08. You now have $208.08 in savings—an extra $0.08 resulting from the fact that interest was computed more often. If the bank computed your interest every month, it would result in a bit more interest paid.

INVESTING MONEY

Computing interest on top of other interest is called **compounding the interest**, and you may see it in advertisements as "6% interest, compounded quarterly" (it's called a **quarter** because it's one-fourth of a year). This would be an interest rate of 6% per year, computed every three months. You can see from the example just given that the more frequently the interest is compounded, the more interest you earn.

The total amount of interest you get on savings obviously depends on how long you leave the money there.

Problem #1

a) You put $500.00 in the bank for one year at 1.5% annual interest. How much money do you have at the end of the year?

b) How much would you have if you put $1100.00 in the bank for a year at .6% annual interest?

INFLATION

There's another factor to be aware of when investing. **Inflation** occurs when an amount of money becomes worth less every year. An inflation rate of 1%, for example, means that each year it takes about 1% more money to buy the same thing. If a loaf of bread costs $5.00 in the United States in 2025, and there was an inflation rate of 1% it would likely cost $5.05 in 2026.

What does inflation have to do with savings? If you have your money in a savings account at 2% interest, then the $100 you put into savings at the beginning of the year will be $102.00 at the end of the year. With 1% inflation, however, it takes $101.00 to buy what you could have bought for $100 earlier. Thus inflation might be a factor in long-term investment plans.

Chapter 4
Figuring Out Interest

Banks usually calculate interest using computers, but occasionally situations arise in life where you will want to to calculate interest yourself. Here are the basic interest formulas to use for those times.

COMPUTING SIMPLE INTEREST

This is the formula that is used when money is deposited for a known period and interest is computed once, at the end of that time. This type of interest is called **simple interest.**

$$I = Prt$$

I = interest earned

P = principal (amount put into savings)

r = interest rate per period of time

t = number of time periods

$600 is deposited for 6 months at an interest rate of 3% per year, often called per annum. How much interest is earned?

$$I = 600 \cdot 0.03 \cdot \tfrac{1}{2} = \$9.00$$

The total amount in savings at the end of 6 months would be the principal, $600, plus the interest of $9.00, equaling $609.00.

FIGURING OUT INTEREST

The formula for the new amount of savings (S) is the principal plus the principal times the rate times the time.

$$S = P(1 + rt)$$

Exercise 1

Using a calculator (or a spreadsheet, if you would like) calculate the total amount of money you will save in each case.

1. $600 put into a savings account for 12 months at .1% annual interest. If you're using a spreadsheet, the formula is =600*(1+.001)

2. $500 put into a savings account for 12 months at .5% annual interest.

3. $700 put into a savings account for 12 months at 1.2% annual interest.

INTEREST COMPOUNDED ANNUALLY

The following formula is used when an amount of money is saved for a certain number of years. The interest is computed and added to the account at the end of every year.

$$S = P(1 + r)^n$$

n = number of years the money is saved

$600 is put into a savings account at 7% interest and left there for 5 years. How much money is accumulated in the account?

$$S = 600(1 + 0.07)^5 = \$841.53$$

FIGURING OUT INTEREST

Exercise 2

Using a calculator or spreadsheet, calculate the total amount of money you will save in each case.

1. $1000 put into a savings account for 2 years at 5% annual interest, compounded annually.

2. $800 for 3 years at 2% annual interest, compounded annually.

3. $1200 for 3 years at 3% annual interest, compounded annually.

COMPOUND INTEREST WITH SAVINGS ADDED ANNUALLY

Here is the formula used when a given sum, P, is deposited at the beginning of each year for a number of years and the interest is compounded yearly.

$$S = P\{(1 + r)^1 + (1 + r)^2 + (1 + r)^3 + \ldots + (1 + r)^n\}$$

… means fill in the rest of the terms, with the exponent increasing by 1 each time until it is equal to n, the total number of years money is saved. The symbols { } are used like parentheses to show that the sum of all the terms is multiplied by P.

$600 is deposited into a savings account each year for 5 years, at an interest rate of 7% compounded annually. How much money is accumulated?

$$S = 600\{(1.07)^1 + (1.07)^2 + (1.07)^3 + (1.07)^4 + (1.07)^5\}$$
$$= 600(1.07 + 1.145 + 1.225 + 1.311 + 1.403)$$
$$= 600(6.154) = \$3{,}692.40$$

If the money had not been earning interest, but simply stored somewhere, the total accumulated would have been only $3000.

FIGURING OUT INTEREST

INTEREST COMPOUNDED OTHER THAN ANNUALLY

Interest is often compounded more frequently than once a year. It might be compounded quarterly (every three months), monthly, or even daily. Here is the formula to use in that case.

$$S = P(1 + r/q)^{nq}$$

n = the number of years

q = the number of times per year the interest is compounded

$600 is put into a savings account which pays 7% annual interest, compounded quarterly. How much is accumulated in 5 years?

Since interest is compounded 4 times a year, $q = 4$.

$$S = 600(1 + \frac{0.07}{4})^{20} = 600(1 + 0.0175)^{20} = \$848.87$$

Exercise 3

Using a calculator or spreadsheet, calculate the total amount of money you will save in each case.

Hint: If using a calculator, do multiple squares.

1. $1500 for 1 year at .05% interest, compounded monthly.
2. $1800 for 2 years at .8% interest, compounded monthly.
3. $3500 for 5 years at .6% interest, compounded monthly.
4. $1800 for 2 years at .8% interest, compounded quarterly.
5. $1800 for 2 years at .8% interest, compounded semi-annually.

FIGURING OUT INTEREST

COMPOUND INTEREST WITH SAVINGS ADDED MONTHLY

This formula would be used if a given sum was deposited each month for some number of years, with the interest compounded monthly.

$$S = P\{(1 + r/12)^1 + (1 + r/12)^2 + \ldots + (1 + r/12)^{12n}\}$$

Suppose you have $50 automatically deposited into a savings account each month from your monthly paycheck, and the interest is compounded according to the above formula. For 5 years the formula would have 60 terms! Using an annual interest rate of 7% again, here is the amount a bank would calculate.

$$S = 50(1+.07/12)^{60}$$
$$S = 50(72.0105) = \$3600.53$$

This total is smaller than the earlier one with savings added annually because the formula assumes you start out the first month with a principal of $50, not $600.

If you started your savings plan with a bigger lump sum than the periodic deposit, another term would have to be added to the formula to take that into account.

For this example, with an initial deposit of $600 total (the first $50 monthly deposit plus an extra $550), the added term would be $550(1 + 0.07/12)^{60}$ = 550 × 1.4186 = $779.68. This would be added to the earlier total for a final total of $4380.21.

Other adjustments to the formula would have to be made if the compounding period were different or if deposits were made on a different schedule. If you made additional deposits to your account at other times, it would also alter the result.

FIGURING OUT INTEREST

Of course, a bank would compute the interest on the actual balance at any time, but with these formulas you could figure out your balance any time. There are also compound interest calculators online if you want to calculate interest automatically.

This is useful for planning or researching ways to save your money so that it earns more interest.

Exercise 4

Using a calculator or spreadsheet, calculate the total amount of money you will save in each case.

Hint: If using a calculator, use the memory (M+) function.

1. Depositing $100 a month for 1 year at .6%, compounded monthly.

2. Depositing $150 a month for 2 years at .6%, compounded monthly.

REAL LIFE

Here are some possibly surprising facts that can be shown using these formulas.

If you put $1,000 in an account and left it there at 10% interest compounded annually for 20 years, at the end of that time the total would be a little over $6,700.

If you put $2,000 in an account and left it there at 10% interest compounded annually for 30 years, at the end of that time the total would be almost $35,000. The interest from that would then be nearly $3,500 a year. That means you could withdraw $3,500 from that account every year without reducing the principal.

If you put $1,000 in an account earning 10% interest, then added $1,000 every year for 20 years, the total in that account would be nearly $70,000. Only $20,000 has been deposited in the account; the rest is interest.

In another 10 years, with $30,000 deposited, the total would be almost $200,000.

At 12% interest, depositing $1,000 a year for 20 years yields a little over $80,000. In another 10 years, that becomes a little over $300,000. The additional 2% interest makes a big difference over a long period of time.

Chapter 5
Borrowing Money

There are lots of ways to borrow money: loans, credit cards, buying on installment plans, and so on.

Usually it costs you money to borrow money, but not always. In some cases, a store will allow you from 7 to 90 days to pay a bill without charging any interest. Some credit cards won't charge interest if you pay off the card within 30 days of the charge. The interest-free borrowing period encourages you to borrow the money.

You usually pay interest when you borrow money, and how much you pay is determined by the interest rate. Whenever you see an interest rate, such as 17.99%, it is an annual rate.

There are a few important things to know about borrowing money and the interest charged on different types of loans.

SIMPLE LOANS

In a simple loan, you borrow a certain amount of money, and pay that back plus interest at a certain time. For example, you borrow $500 for 6 months, and agree to pay it back plus 8% interest.

The formula to use to figure out how much interest you pay is the same one you used to figure how much interest you could earn on a savings account.

$$I = Prt \qquad (\text{Interest} = \text{Principal} \times \text{rate} \times \text{time})$$

BORROWING MONEY

In this case 6 months is ½ year, so the equation is

$$\$500 \cdot 0.08 \cdot \tfrac{1}{2} = \$20.00.$$

After 6 months, you pay back $520.00.

Now suppose you borrow $500 for 6 months, and the person lending you the money wants you to pay $35 interest. What is the interest rate in this case?

To figure this out, you can rearrange the above formula.

$r = I/Pt$ (rate = Interest divided by Principal × time)

So, the equation looks like this:

$$r = \$35.00 / (\$500 \cdot \tfrac{1}{2}) = 35.00 / \$250 = 0.14, \text{ or } 14\%.$$

INSTALLMENT LOANS

An installment loan is a way to borrow money, often for a large purchase such as a house, a car or college tuition. You borrow one lump sum, and pay it back at a fixed interest rate, with fixed monthly payments called installments, and a fixed period to pay it off. Calculating interest on installment loans is more complicated but worth understanding.

Suppose you borrow $1,000 and agree to pay it back monthly over 12 months. Say the interest rate is 18% a year on the unpaid balance, meaning that you do not pay interest on the money already paid back. Your payments would be $91.68 a month. Here is what happens with a payment.

During the first month, your unpaid balance is $1,000. The interest rate is 18%, and the time is 1/12 of a year, one month. So, the amount of interest you pay for that period is

$$I = Prt = \$1000 \cdot 0.18 \cdot 1/12 = \$15.00$$

That means that out of your first month's payment of $91.68, $15.00 is interest and the rest, $76.68, goes toward paying the $1,000 you borrowed. Next month your unpaid balance is $1,000 − $76.68 = $923.32. The interest payment on that balance for that next month is

$$I = \$923.32 \cdot 0.18 \cdot 1/12 = \$13.85.$$

Now out of your next $91.68 payment, $13.85 goes for interest and the rest, $77.83, is paying off the principal. The unpaid balance for the next month is now $923.32 − $77.83 = $845.49.

Continuing this way, one can make up a table that shows how much of your payment goes toward paying the principal and how much is paying the interest on this loan.

Month	Starting Balance	Payment	Amount of Principal Paid	Amount of Interest Paid	Remaining Balance
1	$1,000.00	$91.68	$76.68	$15.00	$923.32
2	$923.32	$91.68	$77.83	$13.85	$845.49
3	$845.49	$91.68	$79.00	$12.68	$766.49
4	$766.49	$91.68	$80.18	$11.50	$686.31
5	$686.31	$91.68	$81.39	$10.29	$604.92
6	$604.92	$91.68	$82.61	$9.07	$522.31
7	$522.31	$91.68	$83.84	$7.82	$438.47
8	$438.47	$91.68	$85.10	$6.58	$353.37
9	$353.37	$91.68	$86.38	$5.30	$266.99
10	$266.99	$91.68	$87.68	$4.00	$179.31
11	$179.31	$91.68	$88.99	$2.69	$90.32
12	$90.32	$91.68	$90.32	$1.36	$0.00

You can see that at the beginning of the loan period the amount going for interest is higher than at the end because the unpaid balance is higher.

BORROWING MONEY

This gets interesting in large loans for long periods of time, such as a loan to buy a house or a car.

Suppose you want to borrow $380,000 to buy a house and pay it back over a period of 30 years at an annual interest rate of 3% on the unpaid balance.

Your payments would be $1602.10 each month.

Let's take a look at how much of that goes to interest and how much pays back the principal for the first year.

Month	Starting Balance	Payment	Amount of Principal Paid	Amount of Interest Paid	Remaining Balance
1	$380,000.00	$1,602.10	$652.10	$950.00	$379,347.90
2	$379,347.90	$1,602.10	$653.73	$948.37	$378,694.18
3	$378,694.18	$1,602.10	$655.36	$946.74	$378,038.82
4	$378,038.82	$1,602.10	$657.00	$945.10	$377,381.82
5	$377,381.82	$1,602.10	$658.64	$943.45	$376,723.18
6	$376,723.18	$1,602.10	$660.29	$941.81	$376,062.89
7	$376,062.89	$1,602.10	$661.94	$940.16	$375,400.95
8	$375,400.95	$1,602.10	$663.59	$938.50	$374,737.36
9	$374,737.36	$1,602.10	$665.25	$936.84	$374,072.11
10	$374,072.11	$1,602.10	$666.92	$935.18	$373,405.19
11	$373,405.19	$1,602.10	$668.58	$933.51	$372,736.61
12	$372,736.61	$1,602.10	$670.25	$931.84	$372,066.36
Total		$19,225.14	$7,933.64	$11,291.50	

Surprising, isn't it? In the first year you pay over $19,000.00, but more than half of that is going to pay interest on the loan. By the end of the year you still have $372,066.36 to pay on the debt. It costs a lot of money to borrow money over a long period, yet most people do it to buy their homes and cars.

BORROWING MONEY

Exercise 1

Using a calculator or spreadsheet, calculate the total payment and total interest paid in each case.

1. You are getting a loan to buy a new car for $30,000 at 3.6% interest for 5 years. The monthly payments are $547.10.

   Total payment =
   Interest paid =

2. You are getting a loan to buy a used car for $30,000 at 17% interest for 5 years. The monthly payments are $745.58.

   Total payment =
   Interest paid =

3. You are taking out a student loan for $25,000 at 2.75% interest for 15 years. The monthly payments are $169.66.

   Total payment =
   Interest paid =

4. You are taking out a student loan for $30,000 at 4.49% interest for 10 years. The monthly payments are $310.77.

   Total payment =
   Interest paid =

5. You get a loan to buy a house at $200,000 at 3.9% interest for 30 years. The monthly payments are $943.34.

   Total payment =
   Interest paid =

BORROWING MONEY

CREDIT CARDS

The loans you get when you charge something on a credit card work differently. The interest rate is usually higher than other types of loans, and the time to pay off the loan is not fixed. If you make only the required minimum payment monthly, it is difficult to pay off a credit card. Here is an example.

Say you have $5,000.00 charged to credit cards at 17% interest. Your minimum payment would start at $124.26 and decrease each month. This table shows what goes toward the principal and what goes toward interest.

Month	Starting Balance	Payment	Amount of Principal Paid	Amount of Interest Paid	Remaining Balance
1	$5,000.00	$124.26	$53.43	$70.83	$4,946.57
2	$4,946.57	$122.94	$52.86	$70.08	$4,893.71
3	$4,893.71	$121.62	$52.29	$69.33	$4,841.42
4	$4,941.42	$120.32	$51.73	$68.59	$4,789.68
5	$4,789.68	$119.04	$51.18	$67.85	$4,738.50
6	$4,738.50	$117.76	$50.64	$67.13	$4,687.87
7	$4,687.87	$116.51	$50.09	$66.41	$4,637.77
8	$4,637.77	$115.26	$49.56	$65.70	$4,588.21
9	$4,588.21	$114.03	$49.03	$65.00	$4,539.18
10	$4,539.18	$112.81	$48.51	$64.31	$4,490.68
11	$4,490.68	$111.60	$47.99	$63.62	$4,442.69
12	$4,442.69	$110.41	$47.47	$62.94	$4,395.22
13	$4,395.22	$109.23	$46.97	$62.27	$4,348.25
Total		$1,515.80	$651.75	$864.05	

You have paid over $1,500.00 and still have $4,348.25 in debt left after 13 months!

You can create your own tables like this using spreadsheet software to analyze any debt you may incur, or you can use online interest calculators.

BORROWING MONEY

RULES FOR SUCCESSFUL BORROWING

The following example shows why the motto for successful borrowing is

> To save money on a loan, arrange for the largest monthly payments you can afford over the shortest time.

Let's use the example of the house loan we talked about earlier ($380,000 for 30 years at 3%). Suppose you decide to pay that loan back in 20 years instead of 30. Then your payments would be $2,107.47 a month. Since there would be 240 months of payment instead of 360, the total amount paid is $505,792.80. This is still much more than the amount of the loan, but by making your payments a little over $500.00 a month more, you have saved $70,963.20 on your total repayment of the loan.

What if you paid it back in 5 years? The payments would then be $6,828.10 a month. The loan would last for 60 months, so your total payments are $409,686.00. That would save $96,106.80 more than the 20-year loan!

Another question is, how much effort is it worth to get a lower interest rate?

Suppose, for example, you could get a 2.5% interest rate instead of 3% on the $380,000 house loan. In that case, the monthly payments for the 30-year loan would be $1,501.46 or a total of $540,525.60 for the loan. That .5% would save you about $100.00 a month and $36,230.40 over the 30 years.

Another rule for successful borrowing is

> Get the lowest possible interest. Even 0.5% can make a big difference on a large, long-term loan.

BORROWING MONEY

Exercise 2

If you have a credit card balance of $2400, the interest rate is 14% APR (annual percentage rate) compounded monthly, and the minimum monthly payment is $36, estimate how long it would take to pay off the balance making minimum payments. Estimate what your monthly payments should be to pay off the balance in 2 years.

FINANCE CHARGES

In addition to interest, the lender may charge other fees for a loan, such as a fee for the administrative work required. The total of all money you pay for a loan, interest plus all other fees, is called the **finance charge**.

Lenders are required by law to disclose in writing what the finance charge on your loan will be, so you can compare the finance charges and required monthly payments of different institutions before deciding where to get a loan.

Sometimes stores or credit companies will offer very low interest rates initially to get you to borrow money from them. They will often raise the interest rate later, and that makes the loan harder to pay off.

Chapter 6
Taxes

A **tax** is money paid to support a government.

An individual living in any kind of community commonly has taxes to pay. In most cases, it is not difficult to figure them out if you understand the terms used.

In the United States, taxes are paid to city, county, and state governments, in addition to the federal government.

SALES TAX

City, county, and state governments in the U.S. are often supported by **sales taxes**. These are taxes paid on retail items as they are sold. Sales tax is a percentage, so a tax of 4% would mean that the customer pays the price of something plus an additional 4%. If the item cost $8.00, then the customer would pay $8.00 plus 4% of $8.00 or $8.32.

Certain items such as gasoline, alcohol, cigarettes, and automobiles may have special sales taxes on them at different rates than the general sales tax.

Other countries have a similar sales tax called Value Added Tax or VAT. The average VAT is 20%, but it can vary. Canada's VAT in 2019 was 5%, and Hungary's VAT the same year was over 25%.

TAXES

Problem #1

You will be taking a trip to Europe soon and plan to spend $1500.00 on gifts for family and friends. The VAT is 20% in the countries you will be visiting. How much money should you bring for your shopping?

Exercise 1

Compute the taxes in each case. You can use a calculator or spreadsheet, or challenge yourself and do it mentally.

1. Sales tax of 4% on a purchase of $9.00.

2. Sales tax of 5% on a purchase of $15.00.

3. Sales tax of 6% on a purchase of $8.50.

4. Sales tax of 8% on a purchase of $22.25.

INCOME TAXES

The federal government gets much of its income from taxes. **Income taxes** are based on the amount of income earned during that year. Most state governments also charge income taxes.

Income taxes are calculated as a percentage of income, but

a) You do not necessarily pay a percentage of your entire income because you can subtract some expenses called **deductions** from the income amount.

b) The percentage is not always the same. In the U.S a person who has a relatively low income might pay a federal income tax of 10%, and a person who makes a great deal of money might pay a rate of 37%.

Because of these and other complications, calculating income tax requires detailed instructions. These are provided by the government.

Usually, income taxes are automatically withheld from an employee's paycheck, so in effect, you're paying this tax throughout the year.

In the U.S. you fill out a **W-4 form** for your employer to determine the amount to be withheld from your paycheck. This form tells the deductions you are taking so your employer and the government know how much to deduct from your paycheck.

Each year employers give every employee a **W-2 form** that states how much the employee earned and how much was taken out for taxes.

After the year is over, you fill out a form called a **tax return** to calculate exactly what your total taxes should have been and compare that to what was withheld from your pay. These returns are filed with the state and federal governments to report your income, expenses, and deductions. This is how you determine whether you need to pay more taxes, or receive a refund because the amount withheld was too much. In most countries, tax returns must be filed every year.

There are several taxes withheld from an individual's paycheck in the U.S., including

- Social Security, which provides retirement income and other forms of insurance.

- Medicare, which provides hospital insurance.

- Worker's Compensation, a state tax that provides another form of disability insurance if you are injured while on the job.

Besides the income one receives for working, there are other sources of income on which people are taxed. For example, if you earn interest by putting money in a bank or another form of savings, that interest is part of your total income which is taxed.

TAXES

PROPERTY TAXES

When one owns land or real estate, in most countries **property tax** is paid to the local government. The amount is a percentage of the value of the property you own. It is the job of an **assessor** to determine the value of a property.

Exercise 2

Using a calculator or spreadsheet, compute the taxes in each case.

1. Property tax on a building assessed at $1,200,000 at a rate of $30 per $1000.

2. Property tax on a lot assessed at $75,000 at a rate of $1.75 per $100.

OTHER TAXES

There are other kinds of tax.

- One is an **inheritance tax**. If you inherit a sum of money, you may be required to pay a certain amount of it to the government.

- Another type of tax you may encounter is the **import tax**. When something of value is imported into the country, a percentage of its value must be paid to the government.

  For example, if you buy an imported car in this country, the import tax will be included in the price you pay. But if you buy the car (or other goods) while you are travelling outside the country, you will be required to pay the import tax when you bring it here.

Part 3
Math for Measuring

Chapter 7
Measuring Different Ways

Of all the ways we use math in day-to-day life, measuring things might be the most common. And because there are different units for measuring things, we often need to convert one unit to another unit. The recipe calls for 200 grams of flour—how many cups is that?

You might well ask, "why not just ask Google?" Well, once you have a basic grasp of how this works, you can confidently just do the math in your head, and you won't have to take the time to ask. And when this kind of math is very easy for you, you can easily check to see that the answer you came up with does make sense and prevent unfortunate mistakes.

MEASURING DIFFERENT WAYS

UNITS

A **unit** of measurement is a standard amount of something. Units are things like meters or feet, kilograms, or pounds, and so on. There are often many different units for measuring the same thing, as shown in the chart below.

Distance	Time	Weight	Volume
inches	Milliseconds	Grams	Cups
feet	Seconds	Kilograms	Pints
yards	Minutes	Milligrams	Quarts
miles	Hours	Ounces	Gallons
millimeters	Days	Pounds	Milliliters
meters	Weeks	Tons	Liters
kilometers	Years	etc.	etc.
etc.	etc.		

Converting these units is simple. Here is an example of converting feet to inches.

There are 12 inches to a foot, which we can write as

$$\frac{12 \text{ inches}}{1 \text{ foot}}$$

To convert 6 feet to inches just multiply.

$$6 \cancel{\text{feet}} \times 12 \frac{\text{inches}}{\cancel{\text{foot}}} = 72 \text{ inches}$$

The *feet* in 6 feet cancels out against the *foot* in 12 inches per foot, leaving inches as the unit of the answer.

MEASURING DIFFERENT WAYS

To convert 96 inches to feet using the same approach, we have

$$96 \text{ inches} \times \frac{1 \text{ foot}}{12 \text{ inches}} = 8 \text{ feet}$$

How about the number of meters in 10 yards? There are about 0.9 meters in a yard, so:

$$10 \text{ yards} \times \frac{0.9 \text{ meters}}{\text{yards}} = 9 \text{ meters}$$

All you need to convert basic units, then, is to know what the correct ratios are. Here is a table showing several of them.

Conversion Ratios for Several Basic Units
1 inch = 2.54 centimeters (2.54 cm/inch)
1 centimeter ≈ 0.39 inches (0.39 inch/cm)
1 foot ≈ 0.3 meters (0.3 meters/foot)
1 meter ≈ 3.3 feet (3.3 feet/meter)
1 meter ≈ 1.1 yards (1.1 yards/meter)
1 yard ≈ 0.9 meters (0.9 meters/yard)
1 mile ≈ 1.6 kilometers (1.6 km/mile)
1 kilometer ≈ 0.62 miles (0.62 miles/km)
1 mile = 5280 feet
1 minute = 60 seconds (60 seconds/minute)
1 second = 1/60 minute ≈ (0.017 minutes/second)
1 hour = 60 minutes (60 minutes/hour)
1 minute = 1/60 hour ≈ (0.017 hours/minute)

(The symbol ≈ means is approximately equal to.)

MEASURING DIFFERENT WAYS

Exercise 1

Using the conversion ratios given in the chapter, make these basic unit conversions:

1. 4 inches to centimeters
2. 8 inches to centimeters
3. 5 centimeters to inches
4. 7 centimeters to inches
5. 3 yards to feet
6. 10 yards to feet
7. 10 yards to meters
8. 3 yards to meters
9. 2 miles to kilometers
10. 4 miles to kilometers
11. 2 weeks to minutes (suggestion: first convert weeks to days, then days to hours, then hours to minutes)
12. 3.5 weeks to minutes
13. 4 feet to centimeters (feet to inches, inches to centimeters)
14. 7 feet to centimeters
15. 4 days to seconds
16. 3 days to seconds
17. 10 miles to inches (miles to feet, feet to inches)
18. 8 miles to inches

MEASURING DIFFERENT WAYS

INVERSES

Notice that the ratio for converting inches to centimeters (2.54 cm/inch) is the *inverse* of the ratio for converting centimeters to inches (0.39 inch/cm).

$$\frac{1}{2.54} = 0.39 \text{ (to the nearest hundredth)}$$

Similarly, the ratio for converting meters to yards (1.1 yards/meter) is the inverse of the ratio for converting yards to meters (0.9 meters/yard).

$$\frac{1}{1.1} = 0.9$$

This is handy, because if you know the ratio for converting one way (kilometers to miles, for example), you can take the inverse to compute the ratio for converting the other way (miles to kilometers). You don't have to remember as many ratios this way.

Exercise 2

Using only the data given below, find the conversion ratios asked for:

    1 inch = 2.54 cm   1 mile = 1.6 kilometers
    1 foot = 0.3 meters   1 minute = 60 seconds
    1 meter = 1.1 yards   1 hour = 60 minutes

1. 1 cm = ? inches
2. 1 meter = ? feet
3. 1 yard = ? meters

4. 1 kilometer = ? miles
5. 1 second = ? minute
6. 1 minute = ? hour

MEASURING DIFFERENT WAYS

COMBINED UNITS

Combined units are made up of two or more units. Perhaps the most common combined units are the units of speed.

Units of Speed
feet/second
meters/second
miles/hour
kilometers/hour

The cost of meat in a grocery store is often expressed as dollars per pound (dollars/pound). A working person's wages may be stated in terms of dollars per hour (dollars/hour).

Converting combined units works the same as we already learned. If we know that a car is traveling 40 feet per second, and we want to know its speed in meters per second:

$$40 \, \frac{\cancel{\text{feet}}}{\text{second}} \times 0.3 \, \frac{\text{meters}}{\cancel{\text{foot}}} = 12 \, \frac{\text{meters}}{\text{second}}$$

Notice that the *seconds* part did not change, and we just changed feet to meters.

Suppose we want to find the speed in meters per minute:

$$\frac{\text{meters}}{\cancel{\text{second}}} \times \frac{\cancel{\text{seconds}}}{\text{minute}} = \frac{\text{meters}}{\text{minute}}$$

So we have $\dfrac{12 \text{ meters}}{\cancel{\text{second}}} \times \dfrac{60 \, \cancel{\text{seconds}}}{\text{minute}} = \dfrac{720 \text{ meters}}{\text{minute}}$

MEASURING DIFFERENT WAYS

We could go straight from *feet/second* to *meters/minute* the first time:

$$\frac{40 \text{ feet}}{\text{second}} \times \frac{0.3 \text{ meters}}{\text{foot}} \times \frac{60 \text{ seconds}}{\text{minute}} = \frac{720 \text{ meters}}{\text{minute}}$$

Here are three more examples.

1. How do you convert 5' 6" to meters?

    $$5 \text{ ft.} \times \frac{1 \text{ meter}}{3.28 \text{ ft.}} = 1.52 \text{ meters}$$

    $$6 \text{ in.} \times \frac{1 \text{ meter}}{39.36 \text{ in.}} = .015 \text{ meters}$$

    $$1.52 + .015 = 1.535 \text{ meters}$$

2. Berries cost $4.86 per pint. If a pint weighs 6 ounces, what is the cost per ounce?

    $$\frac{\$4.89}{\text{pint}} \times \frac{1 \text{ pint}}{6 \text{ ounces}} = \frac{\$4.89}{6 \text{ ounces}} = \frac{\$.82}{\text{ounce}}$$

3. If scrap wood for a craft project weighs ½ ft. per pound, how many meters per kilogram is that?

    $$½ \text{ foot} \times \frac{.3048 \text{ meters}}{\text{foot}} = .15 \text{ meters}$$

    $$1 \text{ pound} \times \frac{.45 \text{ kilograms}}{\text{pound}} = .45 \text{ kg}$$

    $$\frac{.15 \text{ meters}}{.45 \text{ kg}} = \frac{1 \text{ meter}}{3 \text{ kg}} = .33 \text{ meters/kg}$$

MEASURING DIFFERENT WAYS

When you have certainty about how unit conversions work, writing out each step may not be necessary. For instance, if you know there are 3 feet in a yard, when you're converting yards to feet, you just know the answer is about 3 times as big.

SUMMARY

You may want to memorize the conversion ratios you think you'll often run into. The key is knowing how to keep the units straight, which gives you a reliable check on whether you used the conversion factors correctly.

Exercise 3

Make the following combined unit conversions:

1. 4 miles/hour to feet/hour
2. 5 miles/hour to feet/hour
3. 400 meters/minute to meters/second
4. 300 meters/minute to meters/second
5. 60 miles/hour to kilometers/hour
6. 55 miles/hour to kilometers/hour
7. 10 cents/quart to dollars/gallon
8. 2 dollars/gallon to cents/quart
9. 100 kilometers/hour to feet/sec (first convert to miles/hour, then to miles/sec, then to feet/sec)
10. 80 miles/hour to meters/sec (first convert to kilometers per hour)

Chapter 8
Useful Formulas

Mathematical formulas are facts or rules that use mathematical symbols to describe relationships between quantities. For example, the formula used to figure the average speed of an object, s, from the distance it travels, d, in a certain period of time, t is

$$s = d/t$$

You might be familiar with this as the **rate formula**, meaning *how fast*. It says that, no matter what the amounts are, the average speed is always equal to the distance traveled divided by the time.

For example,

A car travels 100 miles in 2 hours. What is its speed (on the average)?

$s = d/t \qquad d = 100 \text{ miles} \qquad t = 2 \text{ hours}$

$s = \dfrac{100 \text{ miles}}{2 \text{ hours}} = 50 \text{ miles/hour}$

The rate formula gives a constant or average speed as the answer. For the purpose of the formula, these small variations are smoothed out into an average speed.

USEFUL FORMULAS

The ability to convert units and rearrange formulas is quite useful at times. And the math needed to use some common formulas is often simple enough to do mentally.

RATE FORMULA

$$d = rt$$

distance = rate · time

For example,

Landon travels to work each day at an average speed of 42 miles per hour, and it takes him 20 minutes to get to work. He decides to use this data to figure out how far he travels.

First, Landon must put all the times in the same units, and he changes the minutes to hours

20 minutes = 20/60 hours = 1/3 hour

Now he can apply the formula.

d = 42 miles per hour · 1/3 hour = 14 miles

Another example,

One day Landon gets to work in 15 minutes. What was his average speed?

To compute the speed, he must solve the above formula for rate, r.

$d = rt$

$r = d/t$

He makes sure the distance is in miles and the time is in hours. He knows that the distance he travels to work is about 14 miles, and the time is 15 minutes. 15 minutes is 15/60 hour, or 1/4 hour. So, his speed was close to

14 miles ÷ ¼ hour = 56 miles per hour

USEFUL FORMULAS

Exercise 1

1. Nia drives to work at exactly 20 miles per hour. Rearrange the rate formula and use it to find out how long it takes her to travel the 12-mile distance.

2. Jada leaves home 12 minutes later than Nia but arrives at work at the same time. Use the rate formula to find Jada's average speed.

3. Suppose Nia races to a store one day at 24 miles per hour. Use the rate formula to find how long it takes her to get to the store if it is 10 miles away.

MILEAGE FORMULA

$m = d/g$

mileage = distance ÷ gallons

Bella just bought a new car which is supposed to be able to travel 50 miles per gallon of gas on the open highway. She wants to find out how much it should cost her to drive to her aunt's house 900 miles away. How much gas should the trip take?

She starts by rearranging the formula to solve for g.

$m = d/g$

$g = d/m$

Now she can just plug the numbers into the rearranged formula.

$g = 900/50 = 18$ gallons

Another example is

Bella keeps careful track of how much gas she buys on the trip and finds that to travel a distance of 924 miles it required 19.3 gallons of gas. What was her actual mileage on that trip?

USEFUL FORMULAS

She can just plug numbers into the formula.

$m = 924/19.3 = 47.88$ (rounded to the nearest hundredth)

47.88 miles per gallon

If she had done the math mentally as she was leaving the gas station, and rounded the gallons to 20 to make it simpler, how close would her estimate be? Would it be a safe estimate to use for planning her return trip?

Exercise 2

1. A club has a bus which gets 4 miles per gallon. Use the mileage formula to determine how many gallons are required for the bus to travel 22 miles.

2. Another club has their own bus. If they can travel 50 miles on 1.5 gallons, determine what their gas mileage is. How many gallons would it take for them to travel 125 miles?

3. Nicholas has a car that requires 50 gallons of gas to drive to his friend's house, which is 425 miles away. Use the mileage formula to determine the mileage that his car gets.

ELECTRICAL ENERGY

Electrical power companies charge for electricity by determining how much energy was used in lighting light bulbs, turning motors and so on. To compute how much electrical work is done over a period of time, you multiply the power being used in kilowatts by the time in hours, giving work done in kilowatt-hours.

W = Pt

Work = Power · time

USEFUL FORMULAS

Anthony uses only 40-watt light bulbs in his house. He is going on vacation for two weeks and wants to know how much it will cost him to leave three lights on for the whole time if he pays $0.08 per kilowatt-hour for electricity.

First he computes the amount of energy this would use. Since 1 watt = 1/1000 kilowatts, 40 watts = 40/1000 kilowatts = 0.04 kilowatts. The amount of time in hours is 14 days · 24 hours per day = 336 hours. So, the energy used by each bulb will be

$$336 \cdot 0.04 = 13.44 \text{ kilowatt-hours}$$

For three bulbs, then, he will use 40.32 kilowatt-hours. At $0.08 per kilowatt-hour, it will cost him 40.32 · 0.08 = $3.23.

A similar example:

Suppose Anthony decides he only wants to spend $2.00 leaving the three light bulbs on. How many hours can he leave them on?

First, he must figure out how much energy he can buy for $2.00. If $0.08 buys one kilowatt-hour, then he divides $2.00 by $0.08 to get the number of kilowatt-hours that $2.00 will buy.

$$2.00/0.08 = 25 \text{ kilowatt-hours.}$$

Each of the three bulbs gets one third of that, or 8 1/3 kilowatt-hours.

To figure out how much time this means, Anthony rearranges the formula above to solve for t.

$$W = Pt$$

$$t = W/P = 8\ 1/3 \div 0.04 = 208\ 1/3 \text{ hours}$$

USEFUL FORMULAS

Exercise 3

1. Compute the electrical work required to operate each of these appliances, and the total work required to operate them all, for a month (4 weeks, 30 days):

   a) a steam iron that takes 1200 watts of power and is used 3 hours a week,

   b) a toaster that takes 1000 watts and is used 5 minutes a day,

   c) a hair dryer that takes 1600 watts and is used 3 minutes a day,

   d) a TV set that takes 85 watts and is used 4 hours a day,

   e) a microwave oven that takes 1100 watts and is used 30 minutes a day,

   f) a coffee maker that takes 750 watts and is used 10 minutes a day.

2. The 24-hour radio station KLMR found that their electrical bill for their broadcast antenna last month (exactly 30 days) was $16,200 at a rate of $0.05 per kilowatt-hour. Rearrange the electrical power formula to compute how many watts of power the station broadcasts.

3. KLMR wants to cut their electric bill for the next month to $14,000. If the rate remains at $0.05 per kilowatt-hour, how much electricity can they use in that month? Assuming that the month also has 30 days, to what kilowatt level will they have to reduce their broadcast power to continue broadcasting all day long? If they continue to broadcast at full power, they will have to reduce the amount of time that they broadcast. Still assuming the month has 30 days, for what fraction of each day can they broadcast? How many hours per day is that?

4. Station WSPR spent $3400 one month at a rate of $0.06 per kilowatt-hour. How much electricity did they use? What was their broadcast power (assume a 30-day month)? The next month they spent the same amount of money for 50,000 kilowatt-hours. What was their broadcast power in that 30-day month? What was their rate that month?

USEFUL FORMULAS

TEMPERATURE CONVERSIONS

The conversion of Fahrenheit to Celsius temperatures is done with this formula.

$$C = \frac{5}{9}(F - 32)$$

For example:

The temperature of a sunny summer day in Los Angeles is 95° F. What is this on the Celsius scale?

We just plug the Fahrenheit temperature into the formula:

$$C = \frac{5}{9}(95 - 32)$$

$$= \frac{5}{9} \cdot 63$$

$$= 35° \text{ Celsius}$$

Also,

The temperature of a sunny summer day in Reykjavik, Iceland, is 15° Celsius. What is this on the Fahrenheit scale?

USEFUL FORMULAS

To solve this, we first need to rearrange the formula.

$$C = \frac{5}{9}(F - 32)$$

$$F = \frac{9}{5}C + 32$$

Now we can answer the question:

$$F = \frac{9}{5} \cdot 15 + 32$$

$$= 27 + 32$$

$$= 59° \text{ Fahrenheit}$$

Exercise 4

Convert mentally. What is special about the temperatures in 2. and 11. below? What would you say is room temperature in °C and °F?

1. 68°F to °C
2. 32°F to °C
3. 86°F to °C
4. 70°F to °C
5. 150°F to °C
6. 95°F to °C
7. 25°C to °F
8. 10°C to °F
9. 200°C to °F
10. −25°C to °F
11. 100°C to °F
12. −10°C to °F

USEFUL FORMULAS

RATIOS & PROPORTIONS

A certain relationship between two quantities is a **ratio**, a comparison of one amount to another. It could be a comparison of four green apples and six red apples in a bowl. This ratio can be stated as a fraction,

4/6

or a statement.

4 green to 6 red apples

A **proportion** is two different ratios that equal each other. In math, it looks like this

4/6 = 12/18

For an example, the amount of dry oatmeal that it takes to make cooked oatmeal is proportional to the number of servings you want to make. Suppose it takes 12 tablespoons of dry oatmeal to make two servings. Then it will take twice as much oatmeal (24 tablespoons) to make four servings, three times as much oatmeal (36 tablespoons) to make six servings, and half as much oatmeal (6 tablespoons) to make one serving.

The ratios of amount of oatmeal to number of servings is always equal to 6:

tablespoons/servings = 12/2 = 24/4 = 36/6 = 6/1 = 6

As another example, suppose you hear that the ratio of profit made by a company is proportional to the money it spends in advertising. If P is profit, and A is money spent in advertising, this means that the ratio of P/A is always the same number. If we call that number k, then we have this formula.

$P/A = k$

You could also write this formula as $P = kA$.

USEFUL FORMULAS

We can use this formula in the following way:

The Cutting Edge company knows that its profits are proportional to the amount of money it spends in advertising. Last year they spent $100,000 advertising and made $1,000,000 profit. This year they plan to spend $150,000 in advertising. How much profit should they make?

Last year the ratio of P to A is equal to:

$P/A = 1,000,000/100,000 = 10$

Knowing that $k = 10$, the profit for this year is

$P/150,000 = 10$

$P = 10 \cdot 150,000 = 1,500,000$

The profit should be $1,500,000 this year.

Sometimes one quantity is said to be proportional to another quantity *squared*. For instance, the distance it takes to brake a car is proportional to its speed squared.

For d = distance, and s = speed, then

$d/s^2 = k$ You could also write this formula as $d = ks^2$.

Suppose you find out that at 20 miles per hour it takes you 125 feet to brake your car to a complete stop. How much distance would it take at 70 miles per hour?

You use the test result to find k:

$125/20^2 = 125/400 = 0.3125$

Then for $s = 70$, you have

$d = 0.3125 \cdot 70^2 = 0.3125 \cdot 4900 = 1531.25$

At 70 miles per hour, it takes 1531.25 feet to brake to a complete stop. That is over 12 times the distance to stop at 70 mph.

USEFUL FORMULAS

Exercise 5

1. The length of time it takes to type in a computer program is proportional to the number of characters in the program. Vera can type in a program containing 6000 characters in 15 minutes. How long would it take her to type in a program of 8500 characters?

2. Vera sprained a finger and can now type a program of 4000 characters in 20 minutes. How long will it take her to type a program of 7000 characters? How many characters could she type in 80 minutes?

3. The cost of a package of cheese is proportional to its weight. If a package weighing 0.8 lbs. costs $2.00, what is the price of a package weighing 1.4 lbs? How many pounds of cheese is there in a package that costs $4.50?

4. The number of cherries needed to make a cherry pie is proportional to the square of the diameter of the pie. Suppose it took 30 cherries to make a pie 8" in diameter. How many cherries would it take to make a pie 12" in diameter? How big a pie could you make with 120 cherries?

5. The power used by a light bulb is proportional to the square of the voltage applied. If 6 volts causes a light bulb to use 2 watts of power, how many watts would 9 volts cause the bulb to use? How many volts would be required to cause the bulb to use 8 watts?

6. The amount of rubber it takes to make a football is proportional to the length of the football squared. If a football of 12" length requires 0.4 pounds of rubber, how much rubber is required for a football of 9" length? What would be the length of a football made with 2 pounds of rubber?

Part 4
Math for Statistics and Probability

Chapter 9
Statistics

In everyday mathematics, **statistics** are "facts or data of a numerical kind, assembled, classified, and tabulated so as to present significant information about a subject" (*Webster's Unabridged Dictionary*).

A lot of the information we work with in life is in the form of statistics. We hear about employment rates, crime rates, the cost of living, the national debt and other data that is expressed numerically. Statistics are very often used to make a particular point.

By the above definition of "statistic," numbers by themselves are *not* statistics; statistics are numbers which have been "assembled, classified, and tabulated." The numerical data must have been organized by someone and must be communicated to present significant information.

Let's look at some kinds of significant information that can be communicated with statistics.

TRENDS

A **trend**, in this context, means a "general tendency or course, as of events, a discussion, etc." (*Webster's Unabridged Dictionary*). A simpler definition would be *where something is going*.

STATISTICS

To see a trend of numerical data, the best thing to do is to put it on a graph, with time on the horizontal axis.

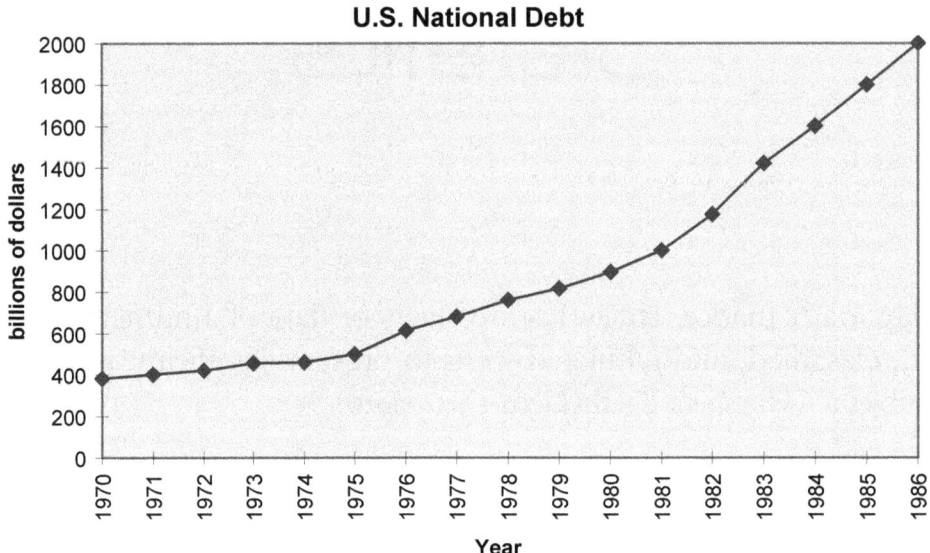

This line graph shows a very clear trend.

When you make or look at a graph of statistics, there are things to think about.

SCALE

The way the graph looks will depend on the vertical and horizontal scales. This graph, for example, shows the same data as the above graph, but on a different vertical scale.

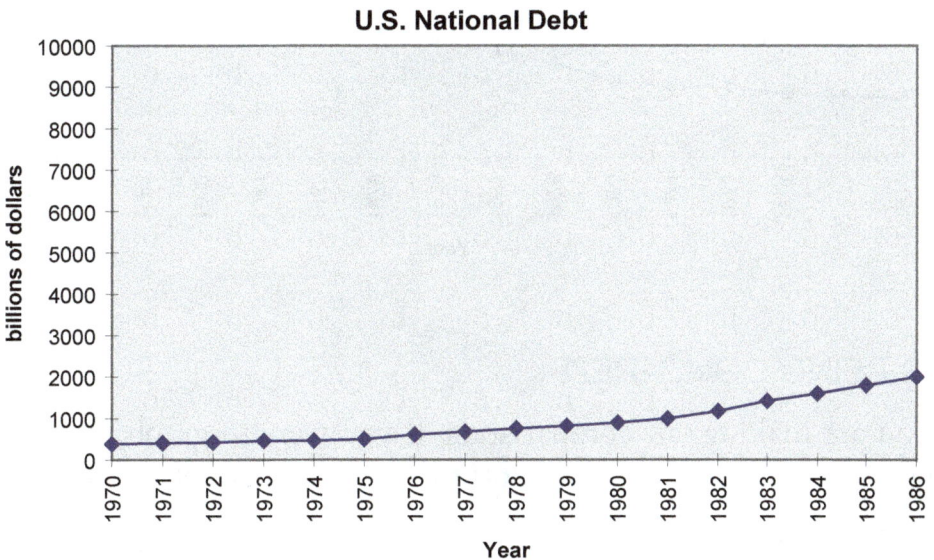

You can cause similar effects by changing the horizontal scale, as the following examples show.

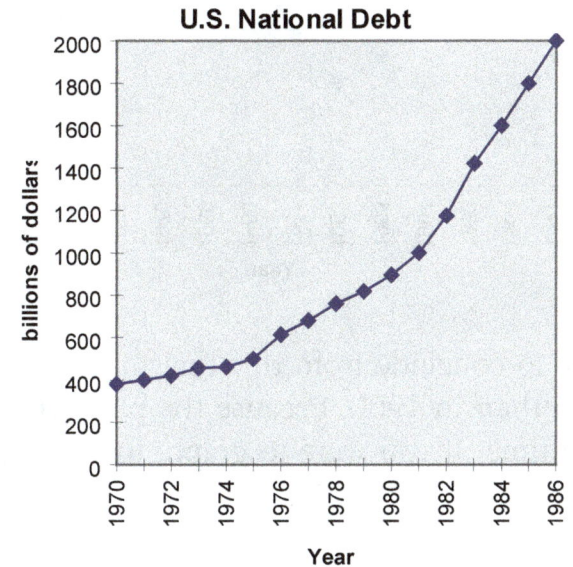

75

STATISTICS

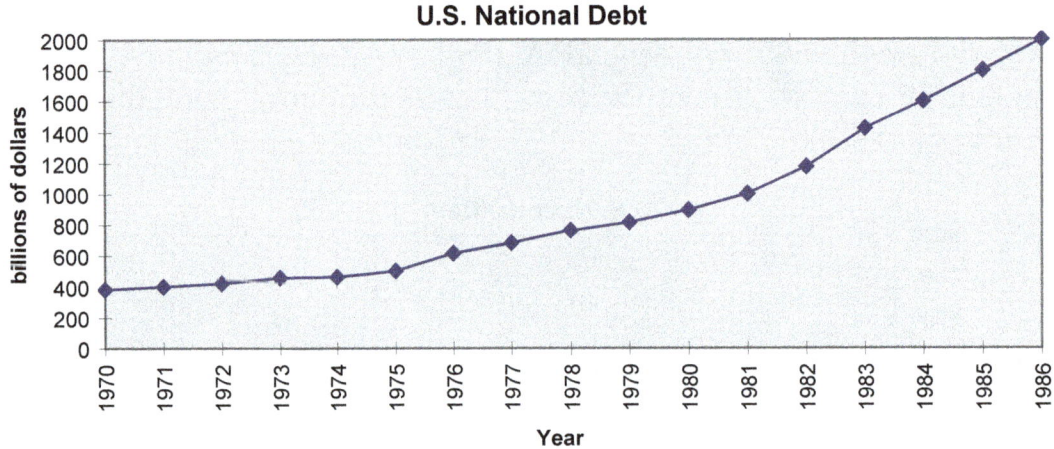

WHAT IS BEING COMPARED

Be sure you are making fair comparisons. If you were to graph the amount of cabbage eaten in America from 1960 to 1975, for example, you might get a graph like this.

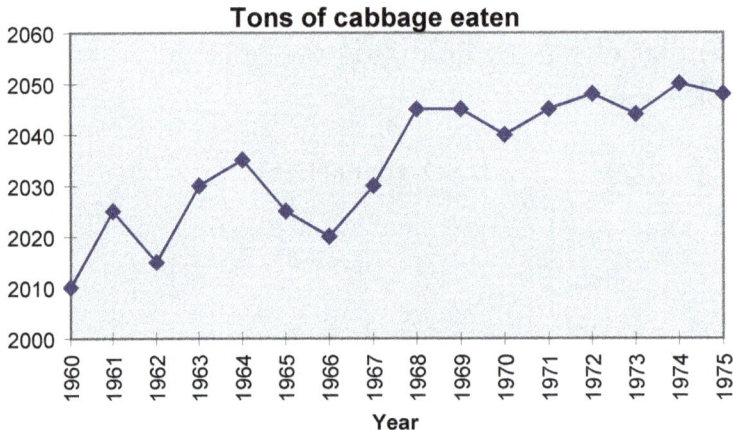

It would be a mistake to conclude from this that most people were eating more cabbage in 1975 than in 1960, because the population was also increasing during the time. If you were to graph, instead, the amount of cabbage eaten per 1,000,000 people over the same period, you might see a quite different trend.

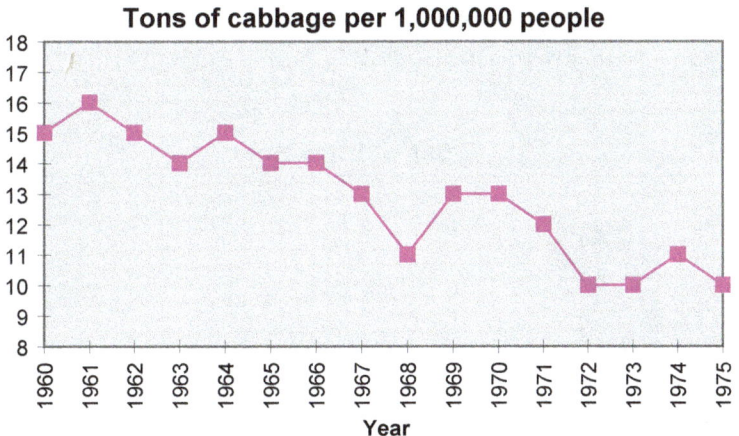

OTHER KINDS OF GRAPHS

Sometimes you are not interested in seeing how data changed over time, but you want to compare it in another way—say geographically. Perhaps you want to know where the most pizza is bought in the U.S., so you can put your pizza stands in a good location. Then you might want a bar graph like this.

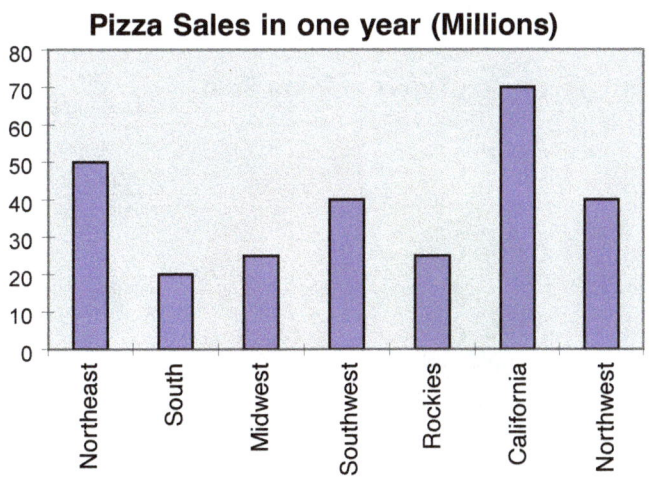

STATISTICS

Maybe you want to show clearly what kinds of pizza people in a certain location like. Your statistical data is that out of 240,000 people who bought pizza in one area last year, 160,000 bought pepperoni pizzas, 50,000 bought sausage pizzas, 20,000 bought plain cheese pizzas and 10,000 bought vegetarian pizzas. You could put this on a bar graph.

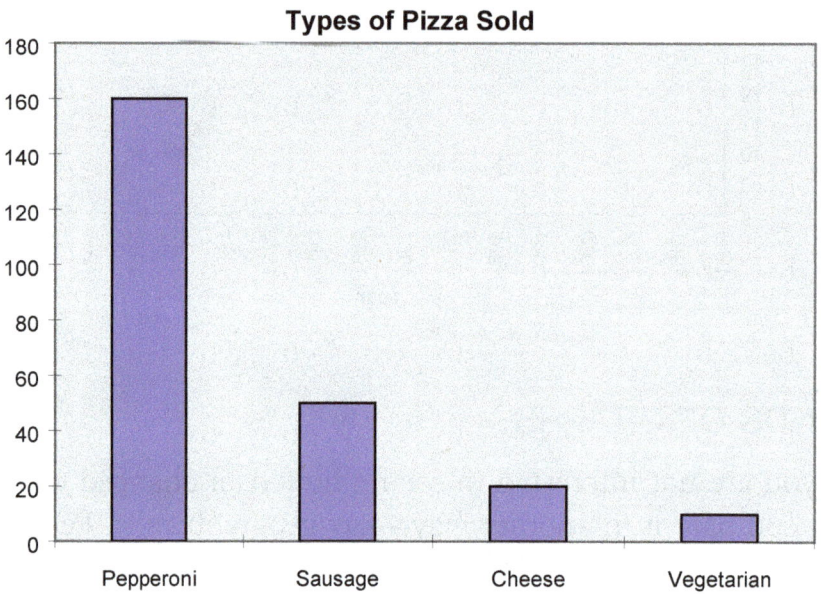

But it might be clearer to show it on a pie graph.

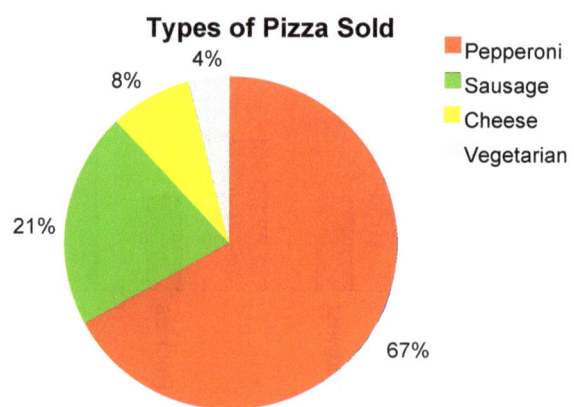

STATISTICS

You can get very creative with graphs, remembering that a graph is an illustration of statistics. For instance, if you wanted to show how peoples' pizza preferences vary over the United States, you might want to make a graph like this:

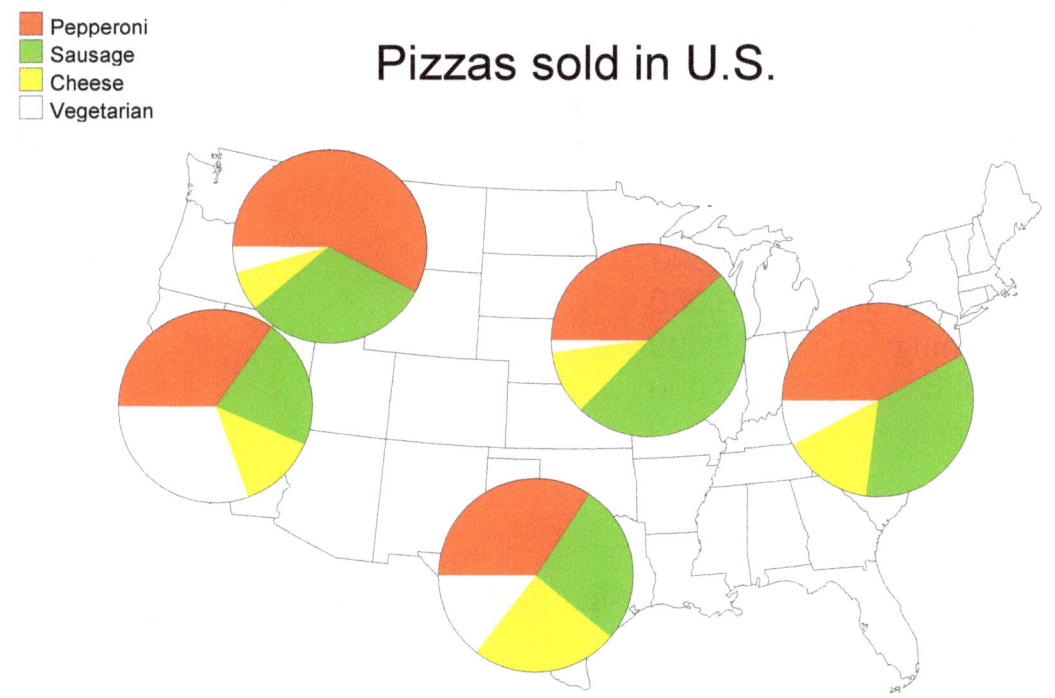

STATISTICS

Exercise 1

Make a pie graph for each of the following sets of data.

1. Survey of 1000 people for their favorite desserts.

   Ice cream: 430
   Pie: 370
   Cake: 200

2. How a family of three spends its yearly after-taxes income of $35,000.

   Housing: $15,000
   Food: $7,500
   Transportation: $5,000
   Clothing: $2,000
   Health: $3,000
   Other: $2,500

AVERAGES

Many times, we see a summary of statistical data rather than all the data.

For example, suppose you were deciding whether to move to Hillwood or Mapleton, and you found the following as data on the average income of families in each of these two cities.

City	Average annual income
Hillwood	$54,000
Mapleton	$67,500

You might conclude from this that the best place to live is Mapleton.

But these figures could be very deceptive. Imagine, for example, that each city had 1000 people, with incomes like this:

# of Families with Annual Incomes

	$15,000	$25,000	$40,000	$60,000	$100,000	$500,000
Hillwood	100	100	300	300	200	0
Mapleton	500	400				100

You see that in Mapleton, nearly everyone makes $25,000 or less per year, while in Hillwood most people make $40,000 per year or more. With this closer look, you might change your mind.

Averages can be misleading. Because of this, there are other ways to summarize a group of numbers. A common one is the median.

The **median** of a set of numbers is the one in the middle. For an odd number of figures, the median is the one in the middle when the figures are arranged in ascending order—the number three in this sequence: 1, 2, **3**, 4, 5. For an even number of figures, it is halfway between the two figures in the middle—the number 3.5 in this sequence: 1, 2, 3, **3.5,** 4, 5, 6.

If you put all the incomes of Hillwood in ascending order, you would have 1000 figures. The 500th figure would be $40,000, and the 501st figure would be $60,000. The median, then, would be $50,000.

Similarly, the median income for Mapleton would be around $20,000 per year.

In this case the median gives you a better idea of what your own income would likely be in the two towns.

STATISTICS

Exercise 2

Find the averages and the medians of these figures.

1. Size of trout in a pond:

   6", 7", 6", 8", 15", 18", 8", 7", 20", 5"

2. Age of people working in a company:

   25, 35, 27, 42, 50, 38, 21, 26, 45, 33

3. Population of counties of North Dakota:

3,584	4,229	1,138
13,960	3,822	88,247
7,944	54,811	9,338

ERRORS IN THE DATA

Finally, no measurement is completely exact, and some may be very far from exact.

When you want to be careful about how exact a measurement is, you will say how much it might be off in either direction.

Look at this measurement of the length of a pencil, using a centimeter ruler.

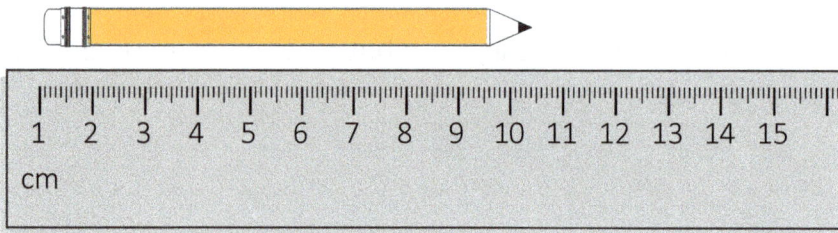

You might say the pencil is 10cm long, but it is actually just closer to 10 than 9. In fact, you could also call *this* pencil 10cm long, because it's closer to 10 than 11:

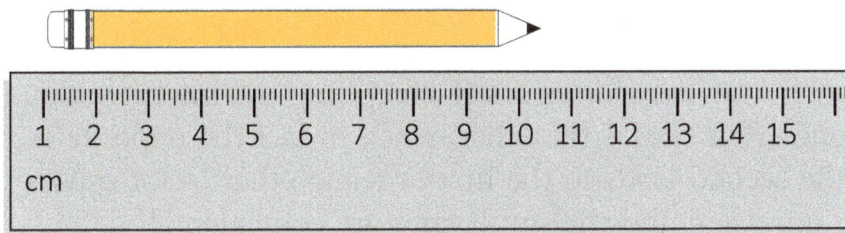

To be accurate, then, you could say that the pencil is 10 centimeters "give or take half a centimeter"—that means it is anywhere from 9.5 to 10.5 centimeters.

Often the possible error in a measurement is converted into a percentage. For example, 0.5 is 5% of 10, so the above measurement could be expressed as "10cm plus or minus 5%."

There may be errors in measurement, and if you're not being told how much the error might be, you could be misled.

For example, you might hear that in 1970 the employment in the U.S. was 90% (of the adult population under 65 years old), and in 1980 it was 85%. You would think that the percentage of adults employed had dropped from 1970 to 1980.

But suppose that the possible error in the measurement is 10% of the population. That would mean that in 1970 employment was anywhere from 80% to 100%, and in 1980 it was anywhere from 75% to 95%.

You don't actually know, then, whether the rate of employment dropped, stayed the same, or increased between those two years. So, finding out how accurate or certain the data is is essential to drawing correct conclusions with it.

STATISTICS

CORRELATION

Often you will read or hear about the **correlation** between two statistics, where two statistical trends are compared, and if the shapes of the graphs are similar, they appear to be somehow related.

This is another area where it is easy for errors to creep into the interpretation. It may be stated that one event causes the other, when in fact the opposite is true. It could be that the second leads to the first or some other factor causes both or they are really unrelated and the similarities are coincidental.

For example, there is a trend for the nation's farmers to produce more food, and there is also a trend for the population to increase. But it would probably be wrong to conclude that the increase in the food supply is causing the population increase. It would also be wrong to conclude that it is the increase in population which makes it possible for farmers to produce more food. In fact, another trend shows that there are fewer, not more, farmers. So if there is a cause-and-effect correlation between food supply and population, the simple trends themselves are not enough to prove it, and other factors must be involved.

Statistics can be very useful tools. If you understand and can apply the concepts in this chapter, you will be able to use this tool more effectively.

Exercise 3

Compute the percentage of possible error in these measurements.

1. The weight of a car is 1450 lb., give or take 5 lb.

2. The weight of a bunch of bananas is 3 lb. 4 oz., give or take 2 oz. (Must convert weight to ounces first.)

3. The voltage at an outlet is 110 volts, give or take 5 volts.

4. The age of a rock is 2 million years, plus or minus 50,000 years.

STATISTICS

5. The velocity of the wind is 50 miles per hour, plus or minus 6 miles per hour.

6. The number of unemployed people in a city is 7000, plus or minus 300.

Exercise 4

Answer these questions mentally.

1. In a mayoral election, the incumbent received 97,500 votes, and the challenger received 93,000 votes. Because it was discovered that some people voted more than once, the possible error in vote counting was estimated to be plus or minus 5%. Does the challenger have a good reason to demand a recount or another vote? Suppose the error had been 2.5%? 1%?

2. A quick way to take your pulse is to count the number of heartbeats in 10 seconds, and then multiply that by 6. The accuracy of this is roughly plus or minus 5%. If you measure your pulse in this fashion and compute it to be 72 beats per minute, what is the actual range of values that your pulse could be? Suppose you measure it to be 80 beats per minute? 60?

3. Suppose the voltage at an outlet in your house is guaranteed by the power company to be 110 volts, plus or minus 8%. You have an appliance which should not be exposed to more than 120 volts. Is it safe?

4. Imagine that a chicken egg must be kept at a temperature between 80° and 85°. You measure the temperature of the room as 83°, plus or minus 3%. Is the egg safe?

Chapter 10
Probability

"The chance of rain tomorrow is 20%."

"A child born in this decade will probably live to be 100."

"The odds of winning the lottery are slightly better than the odds of being hit by lightning."

It can be nice to know with mathematical certainty how likely something is to happen. You can always compute that if it's raining at the rate of 2 inches an hour then the water will be a foot deep in 6 hours, but it would be more useful to know if it is likely to ever rain that hard for that long.

The likelihood of an event occurring is called its **probability**.

METHODS OF STATING PROBABILITIES

We talk about probability in various ways.

Often a probability is stated as a *percent*. For example, the probability of a flipped coin turning up heads could be 50%.

Remember that **percent** means "per hundred," so a 50 percent probability of heads means that out of 100 coin flips, 50 of them should be heads and the other 50 would be tails.

What does it mean that there is a 90 percent chance of rain on a given day?

PROBABILITY

It means that out of 100 days that had similar characteristics (temperature, humidity, and so on) to the given day, it would probably rain on 90 of them and not rain on 10 of them.

A 90% probability of rain means a 10% probability that it will *not* rain.

Any percentage can also, of course, be turned into a fraction. Instead of 90%, you could say 0.9 or 9/10, or 9 out of 10.

Sometimes probabilities are expressed as ratios, called the **odds**. For example, the odds of heads on a flipped coin, as compared to tails, could be said to be fifty-fifty or one-to-one, because 50/50 and 1/1 are ratios which express the same probability. A 90% probability of rain and a 10% probability that it won't rain would be nine-to-one odds in favor of rain. It's nine times as likely to rain as it is not to rain. Notice that the odds ratio is not the same as the percent probability expressed as a fraction or 9 out of 10.

A 40% probability of rain, meaning also a 60% probability that it won't rain would be expressed in terms of odds as 40/60 or 40 to 60. You could also reduce this ratio to lowest terms, 2 to 3.

You can convert a probability from odds to percents. Three-to-two odds of one event compared to another becomes a 60% probability of the first event. Think of it this way: three-to-two odds means that out of five occurrences, three will turn out one way and the other two will turn out the other way. So, the percent probability is three out of a total of five, which is the same ratio as 60 out of a total of 100, or 60%.

Here are a few more examples of percent probabilities and the corresponding odds:

Percent	Odds
25%	one-to-three
50%	one-to-one
70%	seven-to-three

PROBABILITY

Exercise 1

Mentally convert these per cent probabilities to odds.

1. 20%
2. 37.5%
3. 80%
4. 40%
5. 30%
6. 60%
7. 75%
8. 90%
9. 10%

Exercise 2

Mentally convert these odds to percentage probabilities (round as needed).

1. 5 to 3
2. 19 to 1
3. 99 to 1
4. 4 to 1
5. 3 to 5
6. 7 to 3
7. 1 to 5
8. 2 to 5
9. 5 to 2

Problem #1

Odds	Percent (to nearest 1%)
two-to-one	67%
one-to-two	33%
two-to-three	40%
three-to-four	43%

Check these for yourself.

PROBABILITY

COMPUTING PROBABILITIES

The Probability of Two Events Occurring Together

Suppose that you are designing a computer to control the ignition in a car, and you know that the operation of the computer depends on two chips inside it. If either one is working, then the system will function, but if both fail, then the computer will not work and the car won't run.

The manufacturer of the chips tells you that, for chip A, one in 1,000 (0.1%) coming off the manufacturing line is faulty, and for chip B, one in 50 (2%) is faulty. Out of the cars you build with these chips, how many will not work?

Imagine you build 100,000 cars. 0.1% of 100,000 is 100 cars, so you can expect 100 of them to have a faulty chip A. If one out of fifty cars has a faulty chip B, then you could expect that, out of those 100 cars with a faulty chip A, two of them also have a faulty chip B.

So, 2 cars out of 100,000 may have both chips faulty—this is a probability of 0.002%.

If we express the probabilities as decimals, instead of percents, and if we use the symbol $P(X)$ to mean *the probability that X will occur*, we have

P(chip A failure)	P(chip B failure)	P(both failing)
0.001	0.02	0.00002

Notice that

$$P(A \text{ and } B \text{ failing}) = P(A \text{ failing}) \cdot P(B \text{ failing})$$

This is generally true with the probability of two independent events, A and B, occurring together.

$$P(A \text{ and } B) = P(A) \cdot P(B)$$

Another example is

Joe spends a total of 4 hours a week at the cafe, at random times, but always between 5 p.m. and 10 p.m. Sally spends 3 hours a week at the cafe at random times but also between the same hours. Suppose Sally's mother glances into the cafe once a week at random times, but again between the hours of 5 p.m. and 10 p.m. to see who is there. What are the chances that she will see both Joe and Sally there together?

The total number of hours in the week between 5 p.m. and 10 p.m. each day is $5 \cdot 7 = 35$. Joe is at the cafe 4 of those hours, so the probability of Joe being at the cafe at any given time is 4/35.

The probability of Sally being at the cafe at any given time between 5 p.m. and 10 p.m. is 3 hours out of a total of 35 hours, or 3/35.

The probability that both Joe and Sally will be at the cafe at any one instant[*] is $4/35 \cdot 3/35 = 12/1225$, or 0.0096, a little less than 0.01 or 1%.

Assuming that these events are independent and Joe and Sally don't arrange their schedules to be at the cafe at the same time, Sally's mother would happen to see them together at the cafe about one week out of a hundred.

How can you use such probability calculations? Suppose you were Sally's mother, and you happen to see Joe and Sally together at the cafe once every few months.

You could easily estimate how much time either Joe or Sally would be spending a week at the cafe, and during what hours they could be there, and then a little calculation would show you that the probability of seeing them together is very low if the events are independent. This means that the events are probably not independent.

---

[*] This problem is a little more complex than it looks, since the longer Sally's mother looks, the greater are the chances that she will see them together. However, if she looks in for a very short time (say, one second), then this aspect of the problem can be ignored, and the probabilities are as stated.

PROBABILITY

A third example

You are designing a new building for a location that has both earthquakes and hurricanes. Your insurance company tells you they will only insure the building if you can prove that the probability of its collapse during the next 20 years is less than one in one hundred thousand (0.00001). You know that your building can withstand an earthquake or a hurricane, but not both at the same time. The probability of an earthquake strong enough to bring down the building in the next 20 years is 1 in 500 (0.002). The probability of a hurricane in the next twenty years is 1 in 2500 (0.0004). Can you get your building insured?

First you check with a geologist and meteorologist and find that earthquakes and hurricanes are independent events. Then compute

$$P(\text{earthquake and hurricane}) = P(\text{earthquake}) \cdot P(\text{hurricane})$$

$$= 0.002 \cdot 0.0004$$

$$= 0.0000008$$

Since 0.0000008 is less than 0.000001, you can show your calculations to the insurance company and insure the building.

The Probability of Either One of Two Events Occurring

In the last example, suppose you used a poorer design and your building would collapse with *either* an earthquake *or* a hurricane? What is the probability of collapse?

You might expect that this probability of one event or another event occurring is higher than the probability of both events occurring together, and so it is. Let's work out the formula for it.

We'll take a simpler example first, then come back to the building.

PROBABILITY

Imagine you have a standard deck of 52 cards, and you pick one card. There are 13 diamonds in the deck so the probability of picking a diamond is 13 out of 52 or 13/52. The probability of picking a face card is 12 out of 52 (there are 12 face cards) or 12/52. What is the probability of picking a diamond or a face card?

You might think that since there are 13 ways you could pick a diamond, and 12 ways you could pick a face card, then there are 25 ways you could get either a diamond or a face card, so the probability is 25/52. But this would be wrong.

You see, three of the diamonds are also face cards. So, there are not 25 ways of getting either a diamond or a face card. There are only 22 ways, 13 diamonds, plus 9 other face cards.

If you are going to add the probability of getting a diamond, which includes some face cards, to the probability of getting a face card, which includes some diamonds, you then have to subtract the probability of getting a diamond and a face card, because you've counted it twice.

The chances of getting a diamond or a face card, then, are given by this formula:

$$P(\text{diamond } or \text{ face}) = P(\text{diamond}) + P(\text{face}) - P(\text{diamond } and \text{ face}).$$

From the preceding section, you can compute the probability of a diamond *and* a face card:

$$P(\text{diamond } and \text{ face}) = P(\text{diamond}) \cdot P(\text{face})$$

Using the probability of a diamond = 13/52, and the probability of a face card = 12/52, you can carry out this computation.

$$P(\text{diamond } or \text{ face}) = 13/52 + 12/52 - (13/52) \cdot (12/52)$$

$$= 25/52 - 3/52 = 22/52$$

PROBABILITY

Here is the formula.

$$P(A \text{ or } B) = P(A) + P(B) - P(A \text{ and } B)$$

This can also be written

$$P(A \text{ or } B) = P(A) + P(B) - P(A) \cdot P(B)$$

There is another way of looking at this. Take the example of flipping coins. When you flip one coin there are two possible results, either heads or tails, and the probability of each is therefore ½. But suppose you flip two at once? Since the probability of getting heads is ½ for each, you might think that by flipping two at once the probability of at least one coming up heads is ½ + ½, or 1. But this is clearly wrong, since there is one chance in four they will both come up tails (the four possible combinations are *hh, ht, th, tt*). The probability of at least one of the two coins coming up heads is 1 − ¼, or ¾.

Similarly, if you were rolling six-sided dice and rolled 6 of them at once, the probability of at least one showing five dots, would be 1 minus the probability of none showing five dots. This would be $1 - 5^6/6^6$, which works out to about 67%. When there are more than two events involved, to find the probability of at least one of them occurring you compute the probability of none of them occurring and subtract that from 1.

Now let's go back to the building example,

$P(\text{earthquake } or \text{ hurricane})$

$= P(\text{earthquake}) + P(\text{hurricane}) - P(\text{earthquake and hurricane})$

$= 0.002 + 0.0004 - (0.002 \cdot 0.0004)$

$= 0.0023992$

And the car example.

Suppose the car system we discussed earlier would fail if either chip A or chip B failed? What is the probability of failure?

$$P(A \text{ or } B \text{ failing}) = P(A \text{ failing}) + P(B \text{ failing}) - P(A \text{ and } B \text{ failing})$$
$$= 0.001 + 0.02 - (0.001) \cdot (0.02)$$
$$= 0.02098$$

Again, this assumes that the two events are independent.

THE MEANING OF PROBABILITY

Let's take another look, now, at what it means to state a probability. Consider the statement that the probability of a flipped coin coming up heads is 50%. Does this mean that if we flip it twice, it will come up heads once and tails once? Not necessarily. It will often come up heads both times or tails both times. If we flip it ten times, will it always come up with 5 heads? Again, the answer is no. Sometimes there will be 4 or 6 heads or even 7 or 3 heads. But *usually* the number of heads will be something close to 5.

Suppose we flip the coin a hundred times. It will not necessarily come up with 50 heads, but it will *probably* come up with something close to 50. If we flip the coin a hundred times, then do that again and again, we would see that *usually* the number of heads was something close to 50.

When we say that the probability of heads is 50%, it means that if we flip the coin many times, the number of heads we get will most likely be approximately half of the total number of flips.

Similarly, if we say that the probability of rain on a given day is 90%, we mean that if we had a lot of days similar to that given day, and we counted how many of those days it actually rained, the answer would most likely be something close to 9/10 of the total number of days.

PROBABILITY

It is also true that the more coin flips you do, the closer you can expect to come to having the number of heads be equal to 50% of the total. You can test this yourself.

PROBABILITY AND STATISTICS

In the case of the coins and cards examples, the probabilities are based on exact data. There are always two sides to a coin and 52 cards in a deck, so each possible event is equally likely.

When predicting hurricanes, earthquakes or the failure of computer chips, the probabilities are really projections based on statistics. One statistic was the number of hurricanes or earthquakes that happened. Another was how many computer chips failed in a given time period in a laboratory.

Where past statistics are being used to determine the probability of a future event, there is always the question of whether conditions in the future will be the same as when the statistics were gathered. In such a situation the mathematics of statistics and the mathematics of probabilities can get confused, and it takes a clear head to keep them properly separated. Remember, the probability of heads coming up in the toss of a coin may always be 50%, but even so the statistics of a long series of coin tosses will only reflect that in a general way.

Insurance companies compile statistics on life expectancies, illnesses, accident rates, etc. To make a profit, they offer their customers "gambler's odds" based on the predicted probabilities of those events occurring. Everyone must make decisions about insurance, and you must know something about statistics and probability to make those decisions intelligently.

Probability calculations are also used when examining the correlation of different statistics. If the statistics show that the two events occur together more often than probability calculations based on them occurring independently say they should, then it may be concluded that they are not independent and are correlated in some way.

PROBABILITY

It is important to recognize that when probability calculations are used to make predictions based on statistics, the results are only reliable to the degree that the original statistics are valid.

This is just a taste of probability theory. There is much more that can be done with it, but this should be enough to enable you to see that this branch of mathematics does provide a way to describe, compute, and predict uncertainties in our lives to some degree. This may be useful to deal with situations in life as they arise.

Exercise 3

Do these exercises mentally.

1. Find the probability of events A *and* B occurring and of events A *or* B occurring (A and B are independent):

    a) P(A) = 0.3, P(B) = 0.2   d) P(A) = 0.9, P(B) = 0.1

    b) P(A) = 0.05, P(B) = 0.15   e) P(A) = 0.4, P(B) = .04

    c) P(A) = 0.5, P(B) = 0.5   f) P(A) = 1, P(B) = 0.5

2. The probability of event Q is 40%, and of event R is 10%. If they are independent, what is the probability of both Q and R occurring? Of either Q or R occurring?

3. The probability of event X occurring is measured to be 0.12, the probability of event Y occurring is measured to be 0.15, and the probability of both occurring together is measured to be 0.1. Are the events independent? Explain, showing your figures.

Exercise 4

1. Jean is breeding rabbits, and notices that out of every four baby rabbits, 1 is black, 2 are black and white, and one is white. She also notices that one rabbit out of eight has shorter ears than the others. If the color

PROBABILITY

of the rabbits is independent of the length of their ears, what is the probability of a baby being born which is black and has shorter ears?

2. If you live in Sheridan, Oregon, you can expect to see a rainbow on about 10 days out of the year. Suppose your relatives from Phoenix, Arizona, drop in unexpectedly also for 10 days out of the year. What are the chances in any given year that you'll be able to show them a rainbow?

3. Since there are 12 zodiac signs in a year, the probability of someone you meet having been born during the same sign as you were is 1/12. Suppose you go to a party where there are two people you've never met before. What is the probability that at least one of them has the same zodiac sign as yours?

4. William is playing a game with his younger brother, Dante. They each flip a coin. If either coin comes up heads (or both do), William wins both coins. Otherwise, Dante wins. After a while, William's father finds out about the game and makes William give Dante back all the money he had lost. Find out why, by computing the probabilities of William winning and of Dante winning (assuming the flips of the coins are independent and that, for each coin, heads and tails are equally likely).

   If William and his brother flipped nickels a hundred times, figure out about how many flips William probably won, and how much money he ended up with, and about how many flips his brother probably won, and how much money he ended up with.

5. Al is playing a simple card game with Deedee and Max. One draws a card at random out of a deck and turns it up, then replaces it in the deck. Each of the others then turns up a card, trying to beat the first card. Suppose Al, as the first person, turns up a 10. What are the chances that either Deedee or Max will turn up a card to beat him (the card must be higher to win; an equal card loses)? What are the chances that both could beat him? (Hint: first decide how many cards in the deck, out of 52, are higher than a ten.)

PROBABILITY

6. Alex keeps his socks in one drawer and his ties in another. It is usually dark when he gets dressed in the morning, so he just pulls out a pair of socks and a tie and puts them on. If he has 10 pairs of socks, with three of them red, and 6 ties, with two of them red, what are the chances he will end up with red socks and a red tie on the same day? What are the chances that either his socks or his tie will be red?

Chapter 11
Closing

Exercise 1

1. Compute the total amount of money resulting from saving $1500 for 2 years at 6% interest, compounded quarterly.

2. Compute the property tax on a building assessed at $1,400,000 if the tax rate is $35 per $1000.

3. Compute a 8.25% sales tax on a $12.00 purchase.

4. Olivia drives to work at exactly 80 mph. Find out how long it takes her to travel the 25-mile distance. Give the answer in minutes.

5. The length of time it takes to paint a wall is proportional to the area of the wall. Jackson can paint a wall of 100 square feet area in 3 hours. How long would it take him to paint a wall of 250 square feet?

6. Aleta has two 100-watt lamps in each room of her 3-room apartment, and she turns them all on for an average of 6 hours a day. What will her electric bill be for a 30-day month if the rate is $0.07 per kilowatt-hour?

7. Richard works in a large company, and goes to lots of meetings. He has noticed from many examples that how late a meeting actually starts (after the time it was scheduled for) is proportional to the number of people attending the meeting. When a meeting has 5 people, it usually

CLOSING

starts 3 minutes late; when a meeting has 10 people, it starts 6 minutes late, and so on.

Richard has a meeting scheduled for 1:00 P.M., at which there will be 18 people. By how long can he stretch his lunch hour (that is, how late can he come to the meeting) and still be there before the meeting actually starts?

Problem #1:

Suppose you are in your local hardware store and you notice that they are having a special "today only" sale on paint. This reminds you that your house needs painting. You check and find they have the brand and color you want to use. But you weren't expecting this sale, so you haven't made any plans and don't know how many gallons you should buy to paint your house.

You know that your house is about 40 feet long by 30 feet wide and about 15 feet high, with triangular peaks on the 30-foot sides that extend up another 10 feet. Visualizing your house and counting mentally, you determine that there are a total of 10 windows, each one about 3 feet wide by 4 feet high, and two doors, both about 3 feet wide by 7 feet high. You pick up a can and read that a gallon of paint covers about 500 square feet.

First figure the area to paint _____ and gallons needed _____

If the paint normally sells for $15 a gallon and the sale price is $10 a gallon, how much have you saved by being able to think on your feet and figure out the amount of paint you need? Amount saved: _____

If you decide to buy extra paint, how many more gallons can you buy and still pay less than you would have had to pay to buy enough to paint your house at the regular price? Extra gallons: _____

Appendix

Getting Started Exercises 105

Answers to Getting Started Exercises 109

Answers to Problems and Exercises 111

Getting Started Exercises

This set of exercises covers the basic math skills needed to successfully read and use the materials in this book. The answers follow.

Whole numbers

1. 397
    +259

2. 1415
    +595

3. 4,576
    +1,324
    +3,578
    +1,023

4. 234
    −195

5. 1,356
    −576

6. 56,768
    −37,249

7. 345
    × 5

8. 476
    ×25

9. 768
    ×234

10. 8)3240

11. 14)4620

12. 56)6888

GETTING STARTED EXERCISES

Fractions

1. $\frac{1}{5} + \frac{3}{5}$
2. $\frac{2}{3} + \frac{1}{4}$
3. $3\frac{1}{4} + 1\frac{1}{6}$
4. $5 - 2\frac{1}{2}$
5. $2\frac{2}{7} - 1\frac{1}{3}$
6. $3 \times \frac{2}{5}$
7. $\frac{3}{5} \times \frac{5}{4}$
8. $2\frac{1}{4} \times 4\frac{1}{3}$
9. $\frac{4}{5} \div \frac{2}{3}$
10. $3\frac{1}{7} \div 5$

Decimals

1. $1.3 + 2.5$
2. $0.45 + 2.7$
3. $0.008 + 12.4$
4. $3.6 - 1.9$
5. $4.2 - 0.05$
6. $3.7 \cdot 4$
7. $0.25 \cdot 0.033$
8. $2.5 \div 5$
9. $4.25 \div 0.25$
10. $2.4 \div 0.08$
11. Change 1/8 to a decimal.
12. Change 0.35 to a fraction in simplest form.

GETTING STARTED EXERCISES

Percents

1. 20% of 50 = ?
2. 12% of 120 = ?
3. 175% of 80 = ?
4. 10% of ? = 7.5
5. 15% of ? = 30

6. 135% of ? = 540
7. 15 is ? % of 50
8. 5 is ? % of 25
9. 12 is ? % of 150

10. If an item originally cost $50, and is reduced in price to $43, what is the percentage of the discount?

11. If an item is sold for $62 which originally cost $75, what is the percentage of the discount?

12. If an item is raised in price from $12.00 to $15.00, what is the percent of increase?

Exponents

1. 4^2 = ?
2. 5^5 = ?
3. 1.15^2 = ?
4. 3^7 = ?

GETTING STARTED EXERCISES

Algebra

1. Find the value of x that makes these equations true:

   a) $3x = 15$

   b) $x + 4 = 20$

   c) $2x + 5 = 35$

   d) $\dfrac{x}{3} - 4 = 11$

2. In these formulas, use algebra to get the indicated variable by itself on one side of the equation.

   Example: $d = rt$ (distance = rate × time); solve for variable t

   $$\dfrac{d}{r} = \dfrac{rt}{r}$$

   $$\dfrac{d}{r} = t$$

   $$t = \dfrac{d}{r}$$

   a) $A = lw$ (area = length · width); solve for w

   b) $P = 2l + 2w$ (perimeter = 2 · width + 2 · length); solve for w

   c) $V = lwh$ (volume = length · width · height); solve for h

   d) $S = 4pr^2$ (surface area = $4p$ times radius squared); solve for r

Answers to Getting Started Exercises

Whole Numbers

1. 656
2. 2010
3. 10,501
4. 39
5. 780
6. 19,519
7. 1725
8. 11,900
9. 179,712
10. 405
11. 330
12. 123

Fractions

1. $4/5$
2. $11/12$
3. $4\ 5/12$
4. $2\ 1/2$
5. $20/21$
6. $6/5 = 1\ 1/5$
7. $3/4$
8. $39/4 = 9\ 3/4$
9. $6/5 = 1\ 1/5$
10. $22/35$

Decimals

1. 3.8
2. 3.15
3. 12.408
4. 1.7
5. 4.15
6. 14.8
7. 0.00825
8. 0.5
9. 17
10. 30
11. 0.125
12. 7/20

ANSWERS TO GETTING STARTED EXERCISES

Percents

1. 10
2. 14.4
3. 140
4. 75
5. 200
6. 400
7. 30%
8. 20%
9. 8%
10. 14%
11. 17.33%
12. 25%

Exponents

1. 16
2. 3125
3. 1.3225
4. 2187

Algebra

1.
   a) $x = 5$
   b) $x = 16$
   c) $x = 15$
   d) $x = 45$

2.
   a) $w = A/l$
   b) $w = \frac{1}{2}(P - 2l)$ $\quad w = \frac{P}{2} - L$
   c) $h = v/lw$
   d) $r = \sqrt{\frac{S}{4p}} = \frac{1}{2}\sqrt{\frac{S}{p}}$

Answers to Problems and Exercises

CHAPTER 2 MENTAL MATH

Exercises 1-5

Students may check their answers with a calculator.

Problem #1

No, you don't have enough money. The total for those items is $34.01

Problem #2

$56.40

CHAPTER 3 INVESTING MONEY

Problem #1

a) $507.50

b) $1,106.60

CHAPTER 4 FIGURING OUT INTEREST

Exercise 1

Note: The answer is given followed by the formula that should be used for a spreadsheet. The symbols used are those required by most spreadsheets, e.g., * signifies multiplication, not ×.

1. $600.60 = 600*(1 + .001)

2. $502.50 = 500*(1 + .005)

3. $708.40 = 700*(1 + .012)

ANSWERS TO PROBLEMS AND EXERCISES

Exercise 2

1. $\$1102.50 = 1000*(1 + .05)^2$

2. $\$848.96 = 800*(1 + .02)^3$

3. $\$1311.27 = 1200*(1 + .03)^3$

Exercise 3

Answers are rounded to the nearest cent.

1. $\$1500.75 = 1500*(1 + .0005/12)^{12}$

2. $\$1829.02 = 1800*(1 + .008/12)^{24}$

3. $\$3606.56 = 3500*(1 + .006/12)^{60}$

4. $\$1829.00 = 1800*(1 + .008/4)^8$

5. $\$1828.97 = 1800*(1 + .008/2)^4$

Exercise 4

1. $\$1203.91 = 100*(1 + .006/12)^1 + (1 + .006/12)^2 \ldots$
   $+ (1 + .006/12)^{11} + (1 + .006/12)^{12}$

2. $\$3,622.59 = 150*(1 + .006/12)^1 + (1 + .006/12)^2 \ldots$
   $+ (1 + .006/12)^{23} + (1 + .006/12)^{24}$

CHAPTER 5 BORROWING MONEY

Exercise 1

1. Total payment = $32,826.00 = $547.10 * 60

   Interest paid = $2,826.00 (total payment minus principal)

2. Total payment = $44,735.00 = $745.58 * 60

   Interest paid = $14,735

ANSWERS TO PROBLEMS AND EXERCISES

3. Total payment = $30,538.80 = $169.66 * 180

   Interest paid = $5,538.80

4. Total payment = $37,292.00 = $310.77 * 120

   Interest paid = $7,292.00

5. Total payment = $339,602.40 = $943.34 * 360

   Interest paid = $139,602.40

Exercise 2

Answers will vary but should be approximately:

It will take more than 10 years at $36/month to pay the debt.

$115/month to pay it in 2 years.

CHAPTER 6 TAXES

Problem #1

$1,807.00. The VAT would be $307.00 for $1,500.00 of purchases.

Exercise 1

1. $0.36
2. $0.75
3. $0.51
4. $1.78

Exercise 2

1. $36,000.00
2. $1312.50

ANSWERS TO PROBLEMS AND EXERCISES

CHAPTER 7 MEASURING DIFFERENT WAYS

Exercise 1

1. 10.16 cm
2. 20.32 cm
3. 1.97 in ($\approx$ 1.95 in)
4. 2.76 in ($\approx$ 2.73 in)
5. 9 ft
6. 30 ft
7. 9 m
8. 2.7 m
9. 3.2 km
10. 6.4 km
11. 20,160 min
12. 35,280 min
13. 121.9 cm
14. 213 cm
15. 345,600 sec
16. 259,200 sec
17. 633,600 in
18. 506,880 in

Exercise 2

1. 0.394 in
2. 3.3 ft
3. 0.91 m
4. 0.625 mile
5. 1/60 $\approx$ 0.017 min
6. 1/60 $\approx$ 0.017 hr

Exercise 3

1. 21,120 ft/hr
2. 26,400 ft/hr
3. 6.67 m/sec
4. 5 m/sec
5. 96 km/hr
6. 88 km/hr
7. $0.40 dollars/gallon
8. 50 cents/qt
9. 91.7 ft/sec
10. 36 m/sec

CHAPTER 8 USEFUL FORMULAS

Exercise 1

1. Rate formula becomes $t = d/r$, answer is 36 minutes
2. 30 mph
3. 0.42 hrs or about 25 minutes

ANSWERS TO PROBLEMS AND EXERCISES

Exercise 2

1. 5.5 gallons

2. 33.3 miles per gallon; 3.75 gallons

3. 8.5 miles per gallon

Exercise 3

1. a) 14.4 kwh/mo
   b) 2.5 kwh/mo
   c) 2.4 kwh/mo
   d) 10.2 kwh/mo
   e) 16.5 kwh/mo
   f) 3.75 kwh/mo
   total work = 49.75 kwh/mo

2. Power formula becomes $P = W/t$.

   $W = \$16,200 \div \$0.05 = 324,000$ kilowatt-hours.

   Formula yields power = 450 kilowatts, or 450,000 watts.

3. $W = 280,000$ kilowatt-hours for the month. They can run all day at about 389 kw, or they can broadcast about 7/8 of each day or about 20 ¾ hours per day.

4. They used about 56,667 kilowatt-hours one month. They broadcast at about 79 kilowatts the first month and at about 69 kilowatts the next month. Their rate was $0.068 the next month.

Exercise 4

1. 20°C
2. 0°C
3. 30°C
4. about 21.1°C
5. about 65.5°C
6. 35°C
7. 77°F
8. 50°F
9. 392°F
10. −13°F
11. 212°F
12. 14°F

ANSWERS TO PROBLEMS AND EXERCISES

Exercise 5

1. 21¼ minutes, or 21 minutes 15 seconds.

2. 35 minutes; 16,000 characters

3. $3.50; 1.8 lbs.

4. 67½ cherries; 16" diameter

5. 4.5 watts; 12 volts

6. 0.225 lbs; 26.83 in

CHAPTER 9 STATISTICS

Exercise 1

The graphs should look like this:

1.
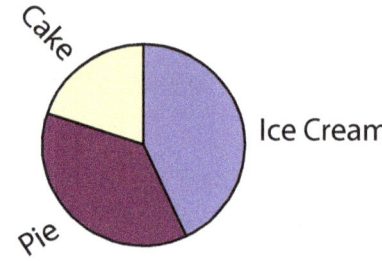

2.
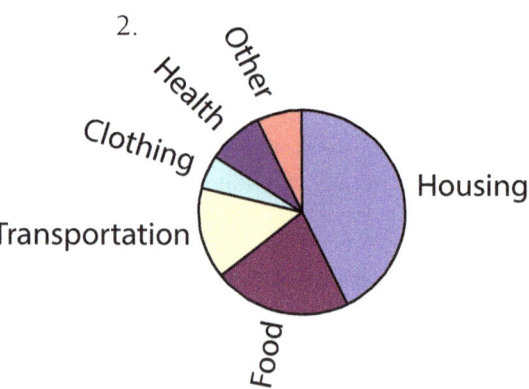

Exercise 2

1. Average = 10", median = 7.5"

2. Average = 34.2, median = 34

3. Average = 20,786 (rounded to nearest unit), median = 7,944

ANSWERS TO PROBLEMS AND EXERCISES

Exercise 3

1. 0.34%
2. 3.85%
3. 4.55%
4. 2.5%
5. 12%
6. 4.3%

Exercise 4

1. 5%: Yes. Incumbent's range is 92,625 to 102,375 and challenger's range is 88,350 to 97,650; challenger could have gotten more votes.

   2.5%: Yes. Incumbent's range is 95,062.5 to 99,937.5; challenger's range is 90,675 to 95,325.

   1%: No. Incumbent's range is 96,525 to 98,475; challenger's is 92,070 to 93,930.

2. For pulse of 72 range is 68.4 to 75.6

   For pulse of 80 range is 76 to 84

   For pulse of 60 range is 57 to 63

3. Yes; maximum voltage will be 118.8 volts

4. No; maximum temperature will be 85.5°

CHAPTER 10 PROBABILITY

Exercise 1

1. 1 to 4
2. 3 to 5
3. 4 to 1
4. 2 to 3
5. 3 to 7
6. 3 to 2
7. 3 to 1
8. 9 to 1
9. 1 to 9

Exercise 2

1. 62.5%
2. 95%
3. 99%
4. 80%
5. 37.5%
6. 70%
7. 16.7%
8. 28.6%
9. 71.4%

ANSWERS TO PROBLEMS AND EXERCISES

Exercise 3

1. a) 0.06, 0.44
   b) 0.0075, 0.1925
   c) 0.25, 0.75
   d) 0.09, 0.91
   e) 0.016, 0.424
   f) 0.5, 1

2. Both = 4%; Either = 46%

3. If they were independent, the probability of X and Y occurring together would be only 0.018. They must not be independent.

Exercise 4

1. 1/32

2. 1/1332 or 100/133225 = 0.00075

3. 23/144, or 0.1597 (to nearest ten-thousandth)

4. William will win 3 out of 4 times, Dante will win 1 out of 4.

   After 100 nickel flips, William will probably have about $7.50 (he wins about 75 times, getting two nickels each time), and Dante will probably have about $2.50.

5. Aces low: Either: 69/169 or 0.408; Both: 9/169 or 0.053

   Aces high: Either: 88/169 or 0.521; Both: 16/169 or 0.095

6. Both: 0.1; Either: 0.53

CHAPTER 11 CLOSING

Exercise 1

1. $1689.74
2. $49,000
3. $0.99
4. 18.75 minutes
5. 7.5 hours
6. $7.56
7. 10.8 minutes

Problem #1

Total area to paint = 2238 sq. ft., requires 5 gallons of paint, savings is $25. Can buy two more gallons and still pay less than the regular price of 5 gallons.

www.ingramcontent.com/pod-product-compliance
Lightning Source LLC
Chambersburg PA
CBHW081617170426
43195CB00041B/2861